The Mountain

A. Alexander Volenski
Mount Rainier

Alexander Publishing
216 E. 10th Street
Port Angeles, Washington 98362-7834

avolenski@lycos.com

Preface

The Mountain—a summer visit to Mount Rainier

The year 1993, camped at the White River Campground, Mount Rainier National Park—this book was generated at the campsite during August and September.

There's a *vastness* to Mount Rainier, emotion and awe, and I hope these recorded experiences will bring pleasure to the reader and also insight into what one can discover while visiting wilderness regions and—the mountain.

AAV

The Chapters
1. Timelines
2. Light Messages
3. Glacier Basin
4. Summer Land
5. Tipsoo Lake
6. Mount St. Helens
7. A Poem
8. Places and People

Timelines Δ

The mountain has a smooth feel to it compared to other mountains I've seen. Soft plush feelings, and upon the silky snow graceful curves are shown that sprinkle the mind with pleasing, even passionate thoughts.

Mount Rainier stands at 14,411 feet, and projects itself with a uniform visual intensity. Grand it rises within a guise of nobility and character as being one of the great volcanoes of the world. It definitely is in a class with Fuji Yama, Popocatepetl, and Vesuvius. Whether in Japan, Mexico, or Italy, these mighty living achievements of shaped terrain, posed in natural formation, are a vital reminder that a presence resides amongst us which possesses superior devastating power. Though Mount Rainier has remained quiet for a long time within a majestically calm beauty, still eruption could occur at any time just as it did at Mount St. Helens over a decade ago.

Tranquil swaying ideas filtered into me while I looked to this mountain and for several minutes I just took in the full view. Where there's snow, a supple and almost totally curved form appears, comparable to what one sees in a beautifully shaped body of the opposite sex. I sensed an alluring attraction, one harmonious provocative even seductive in appeal. There was an enchantment present, something elusive and cryptic like an invisible desire of the passionate kind. As I viewed the stretching ridges near and below the summit where there is mild ermine fleecy snow attached then traced the outline of rocky terrain concentrated like momentary frozen points in time, eventually shifting perspective toward the grand view – mind and rationale became filled with elation and inquisitive wonder. Conceptions and suppositions levitated in mind as animation took hold – the visible impression of Mount Rainier seemed alive as I attempted to bring both essence and visual stimulus together in one pictured thought – the mountains sensation and form is awesome. Time and place, beauty, substance, natural amazement, actuality, all converged within one shape, projecting themselves like colors in a kaleidoscope to dazzle sight and mind with amazement. Inspiration impulsively and quickly realized a vastness that had to be pondered, envisioned, comprehended, and understood, a vastness perhaps even yet to be discovered.

When regarding the mountain as just a mountain and nothing more, I saw the obvious yet at the same time felt peculiar sensations. It was then that I put on a mask of realism and closed off other thoughts. What emerged at that moment was solid rock, ice, snow, blue sky, wind and rain— the mountain was solid, firm, stationary and anchored. 'Beauty comes in many ways,' I mused, 'even mountain nighttime moonlight glow would be beautiful.' This first impression engulfed me and I whispered, "here resides sublimity, a natural form composition—here resides a universal—a natural artistic endeavor—a Cosmic wonder, an expression made manifest!"

A fervor of perplexity flew as upon the wind, quickly and sophisticated it came, and that perplexity penetrated and disrupted my mask of factual. The realism mask was thrown aside, flipped away like a hat blown by an unexpected gust of wind. During that instant I felt momentarily naked and also quite insignificant as humility and truthfulness touched a cord of understanding. The perplexity and sophistication of the mountain generated an inquiry toward the intellect within me, and a strange peculiarity passed over—I wondered, *what is the mystery to behold* – what could it be? The nakedness I felt I knew was motivated by the inner self, indicating the spirit of the mountain could penetrate that concealed domain—ones hidden identity.

The rational and logical, realms which stood firm upon a threshold of actual, began to express there was something I hadn't perceived, a visual dimension overlooked—one yet to be discovered and realized. The inner *psyche* would not let the query of 'the unperceived' free from my mind – that psyche-source reached outward to me and quietly expressed within the silent moment, 'there is more to perceive.'

The Indians refer to Mount Rainier as Tacoma, Tahoma—there are various spellings. Those names they gave to dignified peaks that rise up above all others, and some Native American's refer to the mountain as feminine, some as masculine. That would depend I suppose, upon their own concept and the time and place they were when those names were given.

The bright lofty zenith of the mountain with its airy snow dunes curved and receptive, flexible and adaptable lay in gentle slope and seemed to radiate a feminine spirit semblance. At least I perceive this beautiful peak as feminine. It's difficult to comprehend the size of the mountain as one beholds its splendor. The magnitude, range, and massiveness of terrain, play's upon the human mind's ability to realize proportion. Landscape and sweeping panoramas' one moment appear fixed in deduction and the next moment size and shape elude the calculating sense sending it toward a probing and inquiring domain which contains uncertainty, quandary, and even suspense. The enigmatic magical sensation one may gather from a momentary view of Mount Rainier seems to swirl toward self, and suddenly the query toward the mountain turns into a query of self. A pilgrimage then begins of many paths and miles all presented with an authentic presence*.

In my pleasure to get to know Mount Rainier I traveled from Mount Olympus, the Peninsula, a region of northwest Washington State. My drive too and around Mount Rainier had no timetable, no rush—I took things as they occurred. There were views from many directions, each showing a varied proportioned quality—those features changed slowly as the sun's position moved and I moved. One angle and vista combined with another bringing arousing excitement, a pleasing exhilaration, a multitude of variation—clouds hovering and changing shape, light dimming and brightening, luminous and shadowy both dancing together. Variations of light – depicting round snow packs to focus upon or dark rocky outlines cascading and illustrating, accenting symmetrical shapes curving with snow all presented with various combinations of direction. A collection of adaptations transcended upon the minds visual sense—adaptations sending feeling within an emotional pulse as the sensation of awe does rise and kiss. Passion, alive and real, pure and natural, surged within me as I looked upon the mountain, strong and direct the feel came. A passion similar to when I view a beautiful and sensuous woman; there too I find a-comparable and mysterious appealing quality. Passion exotic and unusual clothed within an aura of wild emotion, beautiful and earthly complete. Passion freely transposing as it reaches to swim within the gentle-confine of embodiment. Passion energetic, endowing and providing poured forth with unlimited delight like

---

*There are a multitude of mountain hikers, pilgrims, that each year visit highland realms, be they climbers, skiers, sightseers, vacationers, clubs, groups—the list is long of those who venture so. One notable said the draw was tremendous, "the mountains are calling me and I must go," John Muir—famous naturalist. John Muir was born Dunbar, Scotland, 21st April 1838; died Los Angeles, California 24th December 1914. American naturalist and author, he made his headquarters in the Yosemite mountain region for a number of years performing a comprehensive study of the geological and botanical features of the Sierra Nevada. He visited Alaska in 1879 exploring north of Fort Wrangel discovering Glacier Bay. Published books: *The Mountains of California, Our National Parks,* and *My First Summer in the Sierra*; also a number of notebooks describing daily notation and written correspondence.

surging creeks and streams of watery ways that tumble from heights above. Aqueous sparkle soothing, embracing, tantalizing, and kissing with organic bliss the meadow hills and forest expanse.

Hiking near, I drank from one of those streams that poured out from above and the water tasted clean and filling like a kiss. A pure soothing taste, and with that sip from liquid fountain a fondness began to awaken within as the spirit and natural character of the region seemed to reach deep inside bringing alive new inspiration and desire, appealing and spontaneous it came to me.

Driving along toward the White River campground where I would stay while visiting, I thought of the many other visitors seen along the way and how they too expressed and conveyed similar if not the same emotion and passion that I experienced. I knew these first impressions, which I observed, were genuinely present and shared by all.

The next morning's dim light of early dawn hovered quietly as light of new day wavered and then brightened. Clear and vibrant I saw Mount Rainier as the warm sun of summer touched its peak. The rising sun came as a radiant sheen of color that covered the entire mountain. A sudden tint emerged as the white snow everywhere began to glow bright pink. That flash of color seemed to grow as though it were a living substance, and as the moments passed the crimson brightened to deep royal pink. Very stunning the pink sunrise glow it seemed unreal almost like an illusion. Then I asked myself in a not too serious way if this spray of color was reality, of course it was, 'for here,' I reminded self, 'lives immense natural beauty', beauty on an original grand scale with unlimited power, a power that it could illustrate. From this phenomenon of pink sunrise glow a doorway seemed to open within my understanding as imagination and subtle reflections raced to gain actuality, and to that entrance I stepped freely without hesitation, for I knew that moments like these with colorful glow upon mountainous stance would not appear often and were rare. This display was like one of those scarce scant moments in life when everything seemed to have met at the right time and place. The doorway I imagined was only present here at this point in time and would not be found anywhere else. This new gateway felt good, and as I gazed to the mountain I began to realize and perceive that an aligned natural sovereignty must truly exist here, one of sternness bold and prominently open. A sovereignty that would utilize every aspect of reflected earthy even wild expression. To me this was provocative and intriguing, seductive and irresistible. I, felt excitement rise as eyes, mind, and imagination seemed to become hypnotized by the plush rosy visual blush being presented. Crimson flame rosiness glow, spectacular redden in a rush of tempered overwhelm, scarlet flush sprayed by light, shining fire of the sun, and I could feel my heart seem to slow into a drifting wild rhythmic dance. 'This is a mountain filled with flaming endurance, perhaps like a flame of love may be with its unpredictability and potency,' I mused, following the thought of glowing flame, volcanic core, pink reflecting sun, even love. I knew I must watch for a parallel, even spirit likeness entwined interwoven here within this design of nature.

The displayed rosy flare upon the snowy peak with its elements in silent illumination, as expressed in these first moments of day came as reflections not harsh or coarse, but as a discreet peaceful manifestation. I rationalized that much truth resided here near the mountain, a truth that one could learn to share-absorb with individuality. This brief contemplation, though momentary, stuck firm in my sensitivity.

While I stood in the cool morning air, observing the pink blush exhibited by the glow of rising sun, a thought came to take a picture of the moment, yet no camera did I have! As that thought to capture on film passed through my mind, traveling the invisible path of perception, a feeling of mildness washed over my body and I suddenly felt warm within the surrounding chill of morning air. Then quickly, as though a lofty blanket or gown of day lifted to block the light, the pink beamed from the rising sun disappeared, vanished. Suddenly the pinks were gone, it was as though these moments of sunrise unanticipated and unpredicted as expressed, were given only to memory. It was then that I spoke, "ah, sweet memory and O' sweet mountain – what can you tell me of your beginning?" At that instant a small cloud mist appeared over one of the huge glaciers and moved rapidly to obscure my observation of those heights, and from that manifested move I knew that the mountain's past and even love would not be granted or shown easily. Coy, shy, tempting, changing, modifying view minute by minute—the mountain seemed vivacious and alive as it stood in complemented fashion with two immortal companions—atmosphere and sun. It was at that moment that my human nature felt a new definable emotion spring free, as though a contemporary passion had suddenly been awakened—an animistic* acknowledgement was established and recognized.

When mid-morning arrived I took a short hike on one of the trails from the campground to have a look around, to familiarize self with the area. The trail I walked led to Glacier Basin and the mountain itself. A few miles up, one will find a left turn that leads to a viewpoint overlooking the Emmons Glacier moraine; moraine, an open path made by a glacier. After taking that turn I reached the viewpoint and saw a wide and long open expanse, an immense pathway gorged out by ice-flows and avalanches that were released by the massive glacier. I walked down into that rubble and debris to do some exploring. As I walked among the boulders and rocky mass I passed by small glacier ponds and felt very alone. Yet it seemed someone was there with me, someone who watched how I moved, I embraced that thought.

The moraine is wide and like a barren landscape with large boulders scattered about in random formation. Small pebbles, sharp and jagged rock, boulders and round stones of all sizes lay everywhere, a place also lacking vegetation—it would probably remain that way for eons. The rocky expanse looked like a huge construction site with dirt and rock scattered, development on a massive scale and who knew how it would look when the glacial slides came again to rearrange. Windswept and desolate this site seemed where only a few small plants and trees grew, yet in a century that could change.

Sitting upon a large boulder, I tried to imagine or gather a glimpse of some of the turmoil that had resided here over time. The moraine I estimated might reach a mile wide, the White River streaming in steady style through its center. Like a giant causeway this all seemed where powerful forces of ice and snow opened, cut, moved, pushed, and tore everything in its path. Relentless upheaval, power vast and unswerving, weight massive and crushing as icy dominion ruled all beneath and near its expanse. Getting up, I walked further into the center of the fragmented moraine and after a ways stopped, it was now midday. Looking up to Mount Rainier and to the left, I saw Little Tahoma Peak, then back to center in the forefront the Emmons Glacier and above it the lofty summit of the mountain itself. All was in full view as I stood, and lifting my hands toward the sky I spoke asking, "please let me know the mystery about you." The sky was clear blue not a cloud anywhere and the crowning summit white and bright. A warm breeze blew against me as it came

---

*Animistic, the belief that natural objects, natural phenomena and the Universe itself, has an actively superior consciousness; pure invisible intelligence, heavens mystic courier, original thought.

down from the ridges there, that evening I had a clear and vivid dream.

There appeared an older woman dressed in white with gray dark color to her hair, like the color of some of the rock upon the mountain. She stood on my left and spoke to a young woman on my right, she said to her, "be careful, for he is Time." We all three walked together as upon the air toward the right for a little way, we were surrounded with whiteness. Then the older woman disappeared, and as I stood still, the young woman moved close to me.

She was dressed in a blue gown like the color of the sky and she smiled at me with a joyous smile, one with a touch of love. Her face was pretty and like the color of the moon, her features rounded and soft, her hair, the color of drifting white clouds in summer sky. She reached out her hand and took mine. As she took hold, she moved closer and I looked into her eyes, eyes the color of deep sapphire blue. I could read her thoughts, loving thoughts filled with a great giving— thoughts of wonder about the man I am and I knew she wanted to share her feelings and I felt pleased.

Then she looked down and likewise so did I, and I saw a white stairway, one with a multitude of steps, which extended downward beyond my sight, and on the right of that stair there was what appeared to be a black handrail. I didn't move from where I stood next to her, yet wondered about the stairway and looked to her feet where her gown touched ankles. The shoes she wore were very unique and unlike any that I have ever seen. Then she spoke to me with her mind and said, "I'm here if you want to reach me." At that moment my sight was transfixed to the stairway and as I looked down that long and endless stair it was then I awoke.

Opening eyes where I lay in my sleeping bag—I saw the dim light of early morning and breathed in the air that was chilled. I recalled the event with the young woman and felt the nip in the air, inside I felt a fever as though my blood were heated, my head felt misty, eyes blurred a little then cleared as I focused. I meditated upon inner thoughts but did not clarify, leaving all open to be all it could be, letting mind float within the meadow of this remembered dream. I hoped the woman dressed in blue with hair the color of drifting white clouds in summer sky would know that I knew and remembered that I was there with her and felt her touch, a warm touch, and that I knew the gentle love she could be.

For now that was how I would leave this conception imprinted upon my mind and reasoning, and as I recalled this event over the days to come, I would enjoy its temperament and embrace all with and as, the mountain, Mount Rainier.

Light Messages ΔΔ

"So it seems," she said,
as we walked in among the rough,
"that you and me
should dream a dream
where few have seen
the stream."

I could not tell
how long it lasted,
nor know where
we might be,
yet in this place
that seemed like space,
I knew we both
were free.

Then as we walked
upon the land
and viewed the greens
so green,
she asked me if
perhaps by chance,
we two might meet
again.

This land on which
we both now stood
was earth and trees
and rock,
and seemed secured within
an absolute,
where awareness
is so true,
and we realized too,
this all
was very new.

T'was different
this site,
yet tangible full,
t'was touchable

actual and obvious,
much like a world
that I did know
secluded beneath
a sky of blue...

This sky was clear
seemed very near,
the air was fresh
and light,
it was as though
we were upon
a sphere of mere
delight.

I looked to her
and realized then,
there were some things
that I must say,
"the real you see
from where I come,
where body, mind, and self,
breathe a while
love a while,
touch and see and do,
is an abode
you may not want
to do the things
you do,
so when you ask me
will we meet anew,
I really cannot say,
for when I awake
from this dream,
it is there
that I will be."

Her eyes were clear
her hand was near,
her mind was open too,
then she moved

and touched my brow,
her fingers warm
so smooth,
and she smiled
and spoke to me
with words
that seemed so true.

"I can tell you this
in truth and love,
your memory I shall hold
within my mind
and inner self,
a love so sweet
yet bold,
and as you dream
I hope to find
you coming here to me,
to share a while
your truth and mind,
to help us both
be free."

I looked to her
and answered thus,
yet few words did I now have,
"as I walk
and move my feet
made to travel time,
your memory shall
remain with me
within
my silent mind,
for as we are
in life complex,
living as we do,
our meeting here
shared with the moon,
shall live
forever new."
She looked at me
as she listened too,
of words and thoughts

we had,
she seemed so alert,
and her eyes were clear
and soft,
her hands so very smooth,
and I yearned to know
much more of her
in form and body too,
yet knew inside
such things as those,
weren't yet for us
to do.

She smiled at me
because she knew,
the feelings that
I had,
and whispered back
into my ear,
"your existence is so dear,
I wish we could be near."

Emotion stirred
within me so,
I felt a tremor
cold,
but did not make
this point to her,
which lingered
in my toes.

Then she said
with a mellow soft voice,
"come with me
if you want,"
and breathing there
where I stood,
I wondered how
I may,
and knew that truth
in of itself
could truly
only say.

There in dream
the land so free
where truth is shared
by all,
some create a bridge
to link across,
to places
that are known.

A site abides
where love resides,
and all are free to go,
if only as
upon the way,
they let
their feelings show.

We beheld our meeting
was meant to be,
our life a plan
to be achieved,
and as we advanced
to meet again,
it's there we shall
both know,
that life as now
as time does pass,
is merely spent
to find at last,
what we
both truly knew...

For hidden in the simpleness
which life seems all to be,
is the heart and truth we have

that speaks to us so free,
and if we listen search and find
what's neatly held within,
we're sure to see within ourselves
the way that's always been,
and come at last
to a realm
which truly always is.

We looked to each
both standing there,
all was so clear and real
senses alive and open,
and as we saw the fading come
as misty air did rise,
we knew this span
of shifting sway,
was soon to send
us both,
to our separate days.

So we two reluctantly
braced for parting so,
and as I released her hand so smooth
she gazed in silence too...

Parting dreams
are hard to do
when love is clear
and true,
but to us both
in memory fine,
this dream would be
infused,
which came to us within the light
of calm and silent moon.

Glacier Basin △△△

It was early morning of another day, again the sky clear and crisp, no-clouds to be seen, the White River campground, quiet, for most were asleep as I walked toward the river to view the mountain. This campground is located on the north side of the White River, which pours east for several miles and then swings north. A small campfire area with log seats is situated there from where one can see the mountain clearly; it is the same area where the National Park interpretive talks are held.

Walking through the campfire area passed many rows of wooden log benches – I could smell the scented freshness in the air, sweet and wild. Then turning to look westward, the view of Mount Rainier loomed snow covered and icy, smooth and ancient, chilling and wind blown, very bright and white, totally bathed in sunlight. As I stood I could look up the Emmons Glacier moraine, it's clear of forest, at the same time I could hear the tumbling turmoil and turbulent upheaval of the White River on my left. The moraine, glacier, mountain, were silent and motionless, the river in contrast, noisy, rushing, surging. This paradoxical combination of the two, silent motionless mountain and roaring surging river were overwhelming; the rivers roar engulfed the surroundings where I stood. Both mountain and river were domineering—they were demanding my full attention. Mind searched, and as it did it locked-on-too relaxed concentration, a site that could deal with the paradoxical.

Suddenly it seemed as though I had emerged through an open doorway, as if a metaphysical domain of the mind had suddenly materialized, encompassing me within its manifested daydream sphere. I swayed and was inundated with emotional thought as though gliding back and forth like a pendulum between grounded reality and positioned projections of the emotionally imagined kind. It was as though I had intersected a void between—a position from which I could observe both reality and imagined at the same time, and I smiled.

The river plunged down from the Emmons with a roar of swirling water created by melting ice and snow being freed from the solid grip of time-locked winters. Water was liberated by summer's warmth, and that ensuing advance of age-old melt brought with it rocks and boulders and earth. The White River is discolored from the grinding of the region by the glacier. The Emmons Glacier with its massive weight from ages of glacial accumulation pressed and crushed everything caught beneath. Its colossal bulk, 4miles long, over a mile wide, with a depth of 225feet just at its lip—is the largest glacier in the lower 48states. I have no idea what it would weigh or the pressure it exerts upon the ground underneath, but it is enough to pulverize boulder's rocks and soil into a fine ingredient the texture of flour. Those whirled with the ice thaw giving the water a color of dishwater, or the tint of ground rye-flour used for making bread. Clouds sometimes have this grayish shade. One can also see such a glow hiking high on dim foggy mountainous days among floating vapors that linger within the melody of nature's misty drift—the alpine slopes and ridges are often found filled with mist.

In my first chapter on Mount Rainier I alluded to the mountain as reflecting the image of a beautiful and stern woman. This morning, August 27th, I looked again for such a reflection and acknowledgment. What I found was something quite different, for as people differ from day to day in little ways that are natural, so too, the mountain likewise varies in its natural expression. As I stood, I momentarily wondered if my persona of the mountain had changed – it hadn't. To me there was still the same feminine and provocative feel along with the delight that teemed with my perception of it.

There are many facets to the mountain which one can relate too as qualities are noted, be they qualities natural, powerful, volatile, photogenic, historical, or just characteristic's relating to the human experience while visiting. The natural habitat and terrain of Mount Rainier is filled with endless assortments, immeasurable arrays in combination. Harmoniously, even melodiously, loom the transforming impressions of color, shape and form, weather, scent, terrain and snowy heights, vegetation, and clear gushing streams natural and complete. Effectively expressed, all is uninhibited, free and original, no manipulated altering—the mountain resides within the healthy sensibility of natural regeneration. 'Natures living culmination,' I mused, a mountain culmination also found within the envelope of one's vital embodied breath and pulse. I reminded myself that deep inside the earth pulses a volcanic flame of a living kind, "a living volcano," as many have expressed.

This copious thought brought a new parallel into view. I breathed deeply the fresh morning air as I heard and looked to the surging White River and metaphorically realized the streaming water of the river to be that of nature's own artery of life. The comparisons and metaphoric theme, which I had just reflected, the natural-world and living world of my body, brought together more clearly an understanding that we all are similar in composition, one with nature.

I began to recognize the flexibility, the unlimited freedom natural surrounds inspire in thought and aspire too in awareness—natural surrounds can draw the hidden, often covered dimension within; inspiring its release into the immediate. Uniquely exclusive and simple, even complex and difficult, is the natural realm. Nature, the universal communicator touches every sense, every nerve, breathing forth and awaking a source reality concealed within us. Realities, which dance with imagination to a melody we are born to enjoy. The wild outdoors with paths of wilderness and the human born to explore, together find true depth and meaning revealed upon this earthy abode. I cherished the uninhabited emancipation, the open-mind and liberty found in the backcountry. A place where independence, that far ranging character within ones own individualism is free to roam.

This morning the surrounding atmosphere, light, time and place, were different compared to yesterday's view of the mountain, but the clear persona of a feminine character I still envisioned distinctly.

I knew I was compelled to pursue that inclination completely. I felt everything at this moment stemmed from my first encounter of the mountain with pink sunrise glow, and coupled to that experience a dream-event followed. Those events came on their own, emerged without preconceived notions. I was bound to them; events I would attempt to bridge together with concentrated thought and strive to be alert to whatever new may arise. Glancing from the river toward the summit, I saw hovering over the top of the mountain a cloud* unlike clouds we see in free flowing sky. The cloud was white and in the shape of an arch, domed and bent, curved like a rainbow would be, or the way an upside down white bowl would appear. That cloud covered the top

---

*Lenticular clouds smooth, round or oval shaped clouds seen singly, or stacked in groups, near mountains. A class of *mountain wave clouds* also called, orographic clouds. The most spectacular lenticular clouds are formed over large mountain ranges.

most part of the mountain and only the summit. The surrounding sky, light blue, clear and void of any other clouds. The upper aery portion of the cloud had a fine dark edge as though an artist had taken brush or pen and lined it in. I felt an ominous intent lingering within that hover cloud as though it gazed down at me. I also felt it had thinking power, impending or even fateful intellect. There was an impression as I let sensitivity fly there of massive power beyond the imagined—potency with command and control.

As I stood gazing, many words came to mind – *appropriate, calm, compassionate, faithful, fierce and gentle, Nemesis thunder, and lightning.* Those words flew like a bird though the meadow of my mind. As I regained composure and called my wandering wits to where I now stood, I attempted to understand that floating cloud and the emotion of the immediate that it seemed to propel. I felt no fear, rather a great urge to be one with it. To glide and soar within its existence as upon a waft of breeze or just be within it's drift and loiter whiteness. The cloud was unusual in its nature—this pearly arrangement with domed hood portrayed in silhouette like halo, and I mused, 'could this be a kind of sacred reflection?' As I regarded that rare configuration no real thought came of the type of cloud it could be—perhaps at the moment unnamed was best. While time passed as I stood—the vapor mist changed and drifted away and vanished. When one breathes upon a mirror a haze appears and after a short while that obscurity evaporates, in similar fashion the cloud also vanished. Now all the loftiness of the mountain was seen – a heavenly approach to the natural surrounds of wilderness. I recalled how a mountain climber had described it—"Mount Rainier is a living alien mass of rock and ice, awesome in character." I would agree, 'it is awesome,' but also much more than just rock and ice. Contemplating the comment of an ascender, someone who had scaled many mountains, I wondered what gender he would place on this peak, of course to me it would always be like a woman. I knew I was caught within an enchantment, a spell perhaps of my own, and captivated as I was with moonlight dreams and daylight visual awe, I knew there wasn't anything I would do to change that nor did I want to separate myself from such an alluring attraction. I preferred to be one with the mountain in all its beauty, magnetism, fascination and charm. The feminine persona that I had affirmed, even if in-dream alone, was still inspired by the time and place of my surroundings, and that natural revealing in all its romantic encouragement I would hold fast too and attempt to embrace completely.

Woman, such a wild and cryptic creature at times, filled with passion, desire, and a drawing wonder to man, is also-matron aspiring to enhance the natural world. A world that must be induced with rationale, cared for, nourished and spared from the brute force of the Industrial Age. Man, a primitive creature born with the primeval spirit, forges ahead in his development of self and his surroundings. The once archaic nature of man has grown into a modern one, but circulating in the blood and linked to the subconscious self is also the ancestral fire. A fire perhaps born out of some form of immortality, as in longevity, durableness, endurance, or simply continuance, I don't have the answer to this question of life and immortality, nor can I speak for another's view on life. While we walk the trail in the forest and climb the mountain, and sometimes follow the path which deer and elk have made over thousands of years, we may often feel renewed in spirit, in mind, and in body. For the fire still burns in our blood that is linked to a far distant beginning, and that fire instills, it rejuvenates renewal to spirit, mind, and body while we are in the wilderness. The nature born in us calls us out, draws us out to be all that we must be, to explore all that we can see and imagine so we may know all that we are as we seek with fortitude to reach our own doorway of truth. A door, behind which we're able to see and know completely who we are, where in the Universe we originate, our capabilities, and—what we really may be.

Woman walks the forest trail—she touches the flower, lupines, asters, and many more that grow in a multitude of profusion flourishing in green meadows, and her inner self feels happy, perhaps even reassured in someway. Man, walks along the stream looking, searching, curious, open to everything as he climbs to see what is there among the peaks. He sees the animals, birds, and fish, and he too feels happy, refreshed and reassured in someway. Together, man and woman comprehend these earthy surrounds, and in their own way know its good as earth speaks to them through individual understanding. Man and woman foster the sweet and sometimes abrupt experience of living as they weather wind, rain, and storm, embraced together sharing their embodied warmth. An emitting radiant warmth flamed by the ancestral fire within the blood—one understands that they must be concurrent in life's duality—man and woman. The collectivity within the human is directly linked to the natural world of which they are born. Man and woman move and are simultaneous as they touch each other, love each other—a giving natural and earthly exquisite, and also sacred.

It was 10AM when I started up the trail to Glacier Basin, which starts at the White River campground. The way is narrow and also wide in some places as it climbs in a gradual lift. The footpath led through a forest showing little sign of fire or tree stumps from the harvesting of timber. Here and there were blown down fir and cedar trees; a wind had marked those spots.

As one walks through the shaded forest it's quiet and dormant in places, barren of vegetation except for the trees, a common reminder of how important sunlight and water are to all growing plants. Hanging from branches of trees one sees Lichens, a combination of algae and fungus clinging and trailing down like a beard on a man or the shaggy mane of an ancient Musk Ox or Wooly Mammoth. The Lichens (USNEA CAVERNOSA) are light green, but now and then I found some the shade of chocolate brown. As I gazed upon the Lichens I felt a thrust or pull back in time, one spanning toward another collective domain as ages of the past seemed to call-out within the lichen – an ancient realm and era could be imagined. 'The Lichens are witness to everything,' I reflected, as I recalled a class in college where the Instructor commented that lichens were probably the first vegetation on earth. If the lichens were first and could speak, much might be revealed about Earth's true beginning and humanities actual significant link with the Earth existence. However, during those college years of my youth, geology and botany, or what came first in nature did not overly impress me for I was more interested in immediate things, girl friends, grades, and how to become rich. Over a quarter century later I find myself beyond that disconcerted phase of youth – a period often caught in a dominating world of obedience for gain at any cost. Today, I sit low on the totem of the monetary structure that towers everywhere, a tower that can isolate, but—also reach to those who are making an asserted effort. There are many questions about man and woman that are unanswered, perhaps even censored by the power of an order; the truth of ourselves must be found and realized to sustain our individual value.

The line of events through the growing nature of living things is significant for it depicts lineage and consistency, an illustrated record that tells the truth of what has occurred, been created and to be created, and also that which has become extinct—planetary catastrophe. Through natural registered factors one can proceed upon a correct course—if true facts are recorded and not withheld. In many ways the naming of things has become a stumbling block, and that, together with censorship has closed off inner perception. When we see a mountain and hear its name, often perception stops as the name sends one off to an isolated thought-direction. Add misinformation or the lack thereof of information to that isolated direction and one's natural necessary perceptive gift to focus suddenly becomes dim—the Dark Age feature. Imagination and subconscious perception were both given to us for a good reason.

The censor that resides around us has become dangerous; we must pursue the removal of such barriers so we can see ourselves truly, individually as we are. We must free our perceptive ability so we may perceive the true individuality we are. A censor could be imagined as a pair of sunglasses worn on cloudy days or in the middle of the night, the censor, characterized by an individual that dons such glasses. How are we to learn the answer to ourselves and the world we exist in if we continue to hide the true nature of self—a nature also comprised of a magnificent language composite—knowledge we were born too perceive. Truly, who benefits from such acts that conceal self? The beautiful individual you are in all your vastness and uniqueness doesn't benefit so concealed. What could be the motive fear surrounding censorship? When a man learns his individual significance as he strives toward completeness, then truth and peace and 'the pursuit of happiness' shall be everywhere. The stream of creation moves in multi-directions and is fused to multiple dimensions. When the truth of our beginning is realized, the mistakes and wrong turns can be adjusted, upheavals smoothed out. We must learn to connect and open our living library of mind, a source we were born to realize and use, a library within us that came with our birth, a library uniquely and individually our own; there are not two libraries alike in the Universe.

Relaxing mind for a moment and still gazing upon the lichens, I tried to picture the past, how some of the lines-through-time, histories, happenings, may have appeared in the immediate surrounding forest. I felt deep foreboding tones like a darkened void, a dark age; there seemed a great aloneness, maybe even grief, but the emotions I couldn't ascertain. The emotion was there, indicating a void with pain, ignorance, transgression, brute force, peace, silence, fire, ash, tremors, SOS, and the Nemesis of nature. As I drifted and pursued these thoughts I looked for light in among the hazy impressions that came to mind. 'There must have been a massive shock wave, continental drift,' I mused, perhaps a cataclysmic land separation*. I needed somewhere to focus. The simplest place at that moment seemed to be books, films and photos of Natural History that I had read or seen. The storehouse of compiled information on our natural surroundings is vast and growing—a true benefit if only for a beginning. One can be heartened by the effort made by Naturalist to bring knowledge of the natural world's heritage to us. One must distinguish how important that work is to help broaden and expand our individual perception. The living-library of the mind is a perception filled with a treasure chest of knowledge waiting to be discovered and opened. The mystery within us is linked to the natural world of which we live; one gathers a little more light through the effort of Naturalist. With such study one begins to link the inner source to the outer shell—a self-reality that arrives with pictured mental clearness. An image-actuality-expression of what really has been, those

---

*Native Indian legend records that Mount Rainier and Mount Olympus originally were side by side, that a black dragon appeared in the sky in day, and became fiery red at night—at that time Mount Rainier moved to where it now resides. That dragon could represent an approaching object, a comet with a whirling fiery tail at night and a black fluxing tail during day—a comet that came near earth thousands of years ago causing a great deluge and continental shift. Such events have happened many times in this solar system and on this planet.

images open the mind, they reveal new horizons of awareness, a glimpse that is not mechanical or a manipulated view and they are true views of awareness describing a reality either of the past or an impending present. A rose is a rose—each rose completely original in blossom, stem and color, and of equal natural value, no duplication present, nor should 'a rose' be censored, altered, or manipulated to be something other than a rose.

The route I walked led out of timber to a small open place on the trail—the mountain with its snow glistened in the sun. To my left or south was Little Tahoma Peak at 11,138 feet. That apex was dark with jagged rock surrounded by snow. Little Tahoma is an ancient volcano; a volcano according to volcanologist that sprayed steam and ash long before Mount Rainier emerged—Little Tahoma Peak, a forerunner of this region? The peak appeared intriguing and curious as though calling, *come up to me.* I stood and gazed at its volcanic pinnacle and wondered of those who had climbed it, what had they sensed as they ascended and sweated, what were their thoughts within the imaginative self at the time? What was the climb like, was it difficult and cold or pleasant sunny and warm, and how did that Tahoma apogee appear to them with its attachment to what laid above, perhaps someday these momentary questions will be answered.

During the winter of 1963—a portion of the north side of Little Tahoma broke away and slid down the mountain for several miles. Seven sections of mountain fell in individual sequences and traveled along to the Hummocky End Moraine. Little Tahoma is on the south side of the Emmons Glacier from which the White River surges. The fragmented rocks from Little Tahoma coasted, some even floated on air cushions for a considerable distance down the large White River valley— as the avalanche fell and heaped it covered existing ice and snow in a path that reached 1500feet in width. One can only imagine what it would have been like to witness that massive break away of sliding shifting terrain. An immense side of mountain, falling, cascading and plunging 4000feet; flat layer slabs sailing on muffled compressed air like giant discs soaring, gliding to meet the ground below. Air softening impact here and there, as momentum increased the disc slabs speed sending tons of rock and dirt—heaving mountain forward with thundering sound and turbulence. Meager creatures we are when it comes to that colossal disruptive force—yet, that hidden volcanic power seems to slumber so calmly and peacefully within the gentle realm of nature.

I continued hiking along the trail that led into the forest, shady columns of shadowy green— sunbeams shown through here and there. While I meandered along I spied a hummingbird sipping sweet nectar from a crimson Sitka Columbine (**AQUILEGIA FORMOSA**); I stopped to watch. The little bird so powerful and quick flying forward and backward in darting fashion suddenly hovered briefly as its intrinsic awareness saw me. It then flew to me to have a closer look, like a sentry it fluttered near my head scrutinizing face and eyes then it zoomed off beyond my sight disappearing into the surrounding canopy of forest. As it went I wondered what message it took with it to wherever messages of such a kind were taken. I continued to scan the surrounding foliage hoping to see that Harlequin character, but it was gone for now. Silently I applauded that miniature spectrum of fluff as it pantomimed in-minuet to Sweet Columbine who is ever faithful to him. And I mused quietly of how passionate ardent bird and amorous flower both were on this warm and calm day.

Gaining altitude, I noticed Asters (**FAMILY COMPOSITAE**) in bloom appearing like little white daisy's clustered together. The faded blue color of that flower seemed purple with a tint of amethyst. Have you ever wondered how all these tender flowers got here? A limitless arrangement of amazement they seem to me. Very delicate, elaborate, intricate they are, as too the bees and butterflies. Flowers and insects are comparable in personality to what imagination and perception would be. Lupines (**LUPINUS**) were everywhere too—they seemed strong and hearty as they grew upon and along that highland trail.

Lupines lupines
everywhere,
what have you
that you would share?

We would share the air
the mountain cool,
we would share the day
the moonlight too,
we would share our songs
of you in tune
if we could sing
like birds all do.

Lupines lupines
all so blue,
what can you tell
that's known by you?

The winters silent
still and white,
the snow blows freely
with delight,
all is peaceful
calm and quiet
as we sleep
through winter night.

And in sweet spring
we come awake
to see the world
and blossoms make.

We feel the warm
and kissing sun,
and know that now
all life is fun.

We breathe the air
and taste the dew,
we see the bees
and love them too.
In all of this
we hope to shine,
like sun above
with endless time.

So as you pass here
on your way,
pause sometime
in thought to find,
perhaps a message
hidden there,
that you may share
with others fair.

Leaving thoughts of Lupines, I resumed the hike that led up over a steep hump, the trail went through an alpine forest which stood in dwarfish style, dark green the trees, a great stillness was present – I lingered there in that shadowy dark to catch my breath. Glancing up ahead I could see the meadow of Glacier Basin, bright sunlight shining everywhere—it seemed that I gazed though a tunnel from where I stood in the dim light of surrounding forest. I proceeded in the direction of that splendid light and felt cheerful.

Glacier Basin, at approximately 6000feet, has a meadow that sweeps up to the side of Burroughs Mountain on the right, and enclosed at one end of that meadow lays a small lake. The lake is shallow, the water clear, deer and elk tracks on its muddy bottom. The elk frequent here in summer, as do the deer, along with bear, cougar, and mountain goats.

I walked out of the forest to the open meadow; everything lay's before you giving a wide view of the distant mountainous ridges. To my right the meadow and lake and towering over the half leaning Burroughs Mountain with its column pillar rock that sticks up like a broken off trunk of a fir tree. Very implausible that mountain seemed jetting up into the air. Glancing to my left and over the edge of a bank next to the trail, I saw flowing water from Inter Fork, a stream that's fed by Inter Glacier in the west. Inter Glacier sits around on the side of Mount Ruth (forefront) a little left of center from the place I stood on the trail, Liberty Cap is high above and ahead like a vanguard to the west. The two mountains, Burroughs and Ruth sit across from each other, the meadow is between. Liberty Cap is higher in elevation and attached to the upper part of Mount Rainier.

When I laid eyes on Mount Ruth, which appeared close at about 8700feet, I couldn't make myself look away; there was something about that rugged chunk of rock which held my attention. It seemed an enigma, a quandary of some sort resided there somewhere near its promontory. I would have liked to sketch Mount Ruth or Liberty Cap, but that would be a project in itself, perhaps sometime in the future it would be done. Liberty Cap was partially covered with concentrated cloud it looked windy up there, windy and cold. Now and then clouds which hovered round its snow plumed peak disappeared, then I'd see the area where a massive breakaway of ice and snow had occurred leaving a huge portion of that side of mountain exposed like a rock wall. The only snow on Mount Ruth that could be seen were small patches shaded from the sun, I noticed ravens and another small brownish bird flying near the top gliding on updrafts of warm air. Every now and then the brown bird would fly close to the mountain and disappear within a deep dark draw that plunged down and then suddenly it would reappear out of the shadows. Very lively and sure it flew as it materialized and surfaced out of that shaded veil of airy span that stretched between us. The sky was exceptionally clear except for a few lingering patches of cloud near the top. There was a soft steady breeze the air clean and scented with sweetness from the surrounding meadow, one knew that here where I stood was really where the region of man and woman did join that exotic remote place high in the snow and ice fields above.

The adventure of mountain climbing along with the invitation and summons—the challenge a mountain has does demand great effort. And after the summit is reached and one comes down out-of or off-of that moon like terrain of another world, the green plush meadows are a welcome site where one can reflect upon their journey, trek, even quest that was experienced on high. One can imagine what it must have been like for those early climbers that reached the zenith over a century ago. There are even bits of clothing or other items one may find buried-covered beneath the snow and ice of that era. One early climber wrote in his journal, "…my hat was blown away by a gale force wind!" That hat tumbled so far and out of sight that it couldn't be retrieved, it would be something to find, a 100year old hat, *a century hat* well preserved.

Taking my shirt off then shoes and socks and lying back on a large rock, I let the hot sun soothe with penetrating energy. Closing eyes, I lay listening to the wind; I could also hear the stream gushing below and the idle conversation of other hikers who were visiting this day. Some of those wayfarers were preparing to advance to Camp Schurman, the departure base camp to the crown or summit from this side of Mount Rainier. Camp Schurman just below 10,000 feet sits close to Steamboat Prow, a large mass of tilted rock easily seen when viewing the mountain from this side at a distance. I lay catnapping – that place somewhere between awake and drift-sleep. A quiet peaceful place of mind where one seems to float through space—to glide from on high, to gently rest their feet on another domain. Listening, I could hear laughter, wind, and the call of Marmot, also the whisper sound of running water. One felt the high spirit and encouragement from those nearby climbers that were preparing to ascend – air had lightness to it – I felt a momentary lift within spirit as though I might drift away on high like a bird. However, the hard and rigid rock that I laid upon poked my back and kept my conscious thoughts firmly down to earth.

It was *high noon*, just after 12:00PM and as I continued taking in the rays of sun, suddenly I heard a low deep rumble like thunder. The sound seemed to move rapidly building momentum as it came until it reached a reverberating pitch, it was then I realized what it was, jet-fighters. I quickly opened eyes and grabbed binoculars to see them as they flew low over me, two military aircraft— Air Force F-16's. Like two darts or missiles they passed screaming through the sky. They banked left over Burroughs Mountain whaling and rumbling as they turned toward the west. These two Air Force jets had suddenly appeared out of the southeast approaching at great speed and I wondered what purpose their presence commanded, who had sent them, what could be their mission? Then they were gone along with their mighty sound wave, weaponry, and sensing devises. The air space around Mount Rainier is restricted to the elevation those two jets were at, why did they fly so low— looking for UFO's? Why else would a Commander send them? It's fortunate that the rumble from their engines hadn't started an avalanche. An avalanche that would place the 60 or more climbers up there in danger—that 'fly-by' could have caused the loss of life, it was totally unnecessary.

Seems that even in high places, one still finds the presence of another type of world, one quite different than the world of which I was sunning myself on a rock. It was then that I realized how controlled this life can be and that at times, important personal times, one often found themselves still caught within the cold grip of the Industrial and Technical World of this society. I wonder—with all the technology whether man and woman have built a fence, perhaps an intellectual kind of enclosure, an entrapment to keep them from knowing their true self. One may wonder, as one matures, of such barriers, the natural human awareness areas that are missing because of what technology has produced. I often find it quite perplexing as I walk through this life and see so much of human value that is missed, and how hard it is to reach a future place where one can truly feel complete. I'm thankful for the sober rationale of the natural world and its contained and continued persistence.

After putting on my shirt, socks and shoes, I strung my pack over my shoulder, took another long look at Mount Ruth and Liberty Cap in splendor, said a silent goodbye to the meadow, pond, and Burroughs Mountain then headed down the trail toward camp and the White River campground.

Summer Land △△△△

The sun shown brightly along the road, it was mid-morning August 31st as I drove from the White River campground toward Fryingpan Creek. I was heading to the Wonderland Trail; the same trail that takes one to the mountainous region named Summer Land, this would be my first visit to that area of the park. As I drove the winding road I could feel the full grasp of Mount Rainier taking hold. A comfortable air of familiarity was beginning to take shape, to form with impression, theme, and expression toward continuity. The harmony of Mount Rainier reached deeply within as though the days that had passed were somehow now permanently woven to my subconscious forming palpable melodious configurations that soared and made contact within the hidden domain, dear *Psyche*. Those configurations once woven, would bound quickly back and forth within the magical realm of identity where they'd eventually seat themselves with consciousness on a fabulous imaginary couch named present-time. Each day of my visit had evolved within a song of its own as steps along the way moved in rhythm dancing to a melody new and capturing. Intriguing the songlines that I followed, their arrangement seemed to open like an endless timeless scroll showing all. Each day's harmony though unique and singular in quality somehow twirled with compatible symmetry to combine and express with a multitude of surrounding compositions. Vast arrays of flower with different shapes and color, bees and insects, birds chirping, tall trees for shade, small shrubs with berries, trickling forest streams, air fresh clean and scented. Such were the proportioned and persuasive patterns I found exploring Mount Rainier's wilderness domain; a dominion and realm where seductive even suggestive emotions were on display along with an exquisite arrangement of receptive eloquence. As I hiked and strolled I let the emotional intensity of the moment free to explore some of what I am—in so doing a fresh awareness began to quicken.

The Wonderland Trail of Mount Rainier National Park extends 93miles around the mountain, circling it completely. It's a popular track that many hikers traverse if they have 10days to two weeks, for it takes about that long to circumvent the mountain. The poetry of the Wonderland Trail I knew would be good reading if ever written.

Today I was only hiking to Summer Land to take in the view and see how it was on high. Mattie, a friend who also was staying at the White River campground had mentioned this hike with a kind of daydream look in her eyes and hinted I should "have a look." The term Summer Land had a nice tone, and though I only found it as a location on the map, still I imagined meadow lays filled with euphoric verse of the pleasant kind; a place to see; a site where imagination might find its way into reality. Yes, inspired emotion could have its day there on high within the pleasant meadows of summer.

As I have remarked already, Mount Rainier when seen from different positions possesses an assortment of expression. I would say the mixture is impressionistic it's like variations on a theme similar to what one might find within their own personality or the personality of a friend and acquaintance. Many natural variables exist as one ambles each day through life. Time, surroundings, place, and circumstance, manifest themselves in a continuum that reflects back to self. Real random patterns emerge as displayed characteristics and episodes meant to season ones inner enclosure. The energy of the natural world, free and filled with many perspectives, can assist in finding new sources of self awareness, but keep in mind, some sources are difficult to comprehend because—they're camouflaged! Our private distinction, a disguised envelope of our own personal self is a source we are compelled and born to explore. And in our own mature seasoning that enclosed portion of clarity within our character speaks to us in a variety of ways. Nourishment for mind and body is found near the sea, in the forest, and often high upon mountain ridges, or near meadow and lake of summer. A sustained potency exists in the natural surrounds that cannot be duplicated, controlled, dominated, or manufactured. The spontaneous and distinctive natural world induces new freedoms that shape and tone even humor our temperament. The natural environment can inspire the realm within self, areas of talent that are features to explore and develop, with such maturity one will find new meaning to their life acknowledgements and that in turn will benefit those they love. One of the specialties of the natural world is to help us clearly understand ourselves, to see clearly the beauty we are, but such an accomplishment takes individual effort. Once that effort begins, our uniqueness becomes excited, exuberant, and reaches to be shared with those we meet. The sharing of thought and discovery is healthy—but in that sharing one must also realize there can be a world within a world when it comes to sharing. Sharing is difficult to define because it's often confused with the act of helping.

Two spring birds help each other build a nest hidden in a warm shady place upon gentle limb of tall tree. Together they share the nest that they both helped to build. They have shared in helping each other. The important thing to realize is that the two small spring birds have also helped each other share. This helping to share is exceptional, important, and usually overlooked; it's different than sharing to help. However, the two spring birds understand and in a way they are ahead of many. The more you understand about sharing and its multitude of variation, the more you will have.

The main highways that lay around Mount Rainier of course only offer limited vantage points where one may view the snow capped-apogee. However, a multitude of views exist as one hikes along a trail or while climbing steep switchbacks that angle over ridges—resting here and there one can behold that frosty snowy peak of impressive mountain in many varied and singular ways. The array one sees emerges and cascades with a timeless strategy of permanence. Substantial, durable, lasting, anchored and correct the mountain reaches as its visual image swirls, twirls, and whirls toward us through the invisible air. And our life, our personality, emotion and promising essence, becomes hearty, formidable and alive with eagerness. There is fascination, a magical alluring visual view, a view here and there that pulls like a magnet—one is inclined to wonder what the attraction is? The mountain's visual image delight's the senses, it tickles and there is eagerness, joy or even mirth—emotion often appears as a form of mental laughter. We shouldn't be deigned that laughter nor overlook where the tickle begins.

The veiled spirit and vigor of the mountain, hidden or unnoticed as it often is, appears to be absorbed by the identity within us just as the soil of earth absorbs a soothing raindrop. Thus, significant messages of nature are absorbed within a dimension of self, messages awaiting our acknowledgment of them. That inspiration arrives freely from the mountain, brushes against us in a small and simple way as it helps us strive silently to define, know, learn, and realize, another amazing characteristic, the emotion of Awesome. Awesome also has a partner named Awe, both unique personalities—enthusiastic, provocative, passionate and part of the emotion realm within us. Emotion can be difficult to define—a domain of much mystery. Who really knows the feeling, power and energetic drive of emotion, a force we have pulsing in us—where does emotion truly originate? We must embrace our emotion and learn to understand it, perhaps that's what the mountain strives to do through a spirited couple, Awesome and Awe.

Take an imaginable moment and consider, can one personify emotion through Awesome and Awe—can linguistic tones clearly present an outer expression of inner feeling? Imagine Awesome and Awe both walking along a trail, and as they do, they suddenly hear a chirping call from Emotion. They glide and soar toward that chirping to make contact. As they do, laughter is heard, human laughter; laughter is a type of emotion too. In hidden form Emotion resides until laughter appears. Is it possible that only through Awe and Awesome healthy emotion emerges? Perhaps they both are only realized recognized within the cognizance of laughter. And when all three, Awesome, Awe, and Laughter, look to the mountain do they too realize even a greater recognition. The mountain has smiled upon them for the mountain transmits power, its vastness reaches to and through everything; without the mountain, emotions and expressions of emotion would not be present. If the mountain were taken away, one would find emptiness, a desert without emotion. There's more one could express on this subject of emotions link to the world, and how it's inspired identified, why it exists, and why it's more powerful at certain locations.

Arriving at the parking area next to the bridge of Fryingpan Creek, I parked the 4X4 Dodge pickup, gathered my gear, locked the truck and walked to the trailhead. It was 10:42AM and cool, the cold air I could feel as it filled my lungs reaching deep into the depth of body; clean pure air.

Fryingpan Creek flows from Fryingpan Glacier, a glacier that lay's against Little Tahoma Peak on the east slope of Mount Rainier. Fryingpan Glacier rises from 7800 to about 8800feet and is elongated horizontally. Above it is Whitman Glacier, which embraces toward the top of Little Tahoma Peak. Fryingpan Glacier some say was so named because it is shaped like a fryingpan, and there are other accounts that claim the name originated from travelers who lost a fryingpan somewhere in the area. Here I paused to ponder for a moment the enigma perceived woven in amongst names and the naming of places. I was sure that there was a better name for that site, but will it ever be known?

Today the creek had a little color from the summer melt effect on the glaciers above. Another day when I was here the water was clear, that day I walked along the streambed to explore and get the feel of this watershed; while there I scooped a handful of mountain water and it tasted quite good. If you're not use to drinking mountain water you should be careful for it can make you sick. I've spent a lot of time in the wilderness hiking and have tasted the water thereof and never been affected by any type of disorder, nor have I had 'mountain fever' as it is sometimes called. A purgative disorder of the digestive system similar to what one may experience from taking too many laxatives. Of course, I'm selective of the stream, creek, or source of water I drink, and have passed many fountains of the wild until one was found that felt good.

The following are some simple rules one may use: the stream must be clear and flowing— never drink water that is pooled or stagnate. The air temperature next to the stream must be cooler then the surrounding air (in summer), one cup's the water carefully—do not touch moss or algae growing on the rocks (living organisms). I usually find a streaming gush and collect the water very gingerly as it cascades to me. I have traveled long and dry many times until I found a place to fit these requirements. This practice of course works for me, but in writing this, I'm not suggesting others do the same; each individual differs physically in some way, thus, do as you feel to be best for you or follow the warnings and advisories posted by the Park Administration.

The trail to Summer Land led through tall timber, very large trees—one sees clearly for some distance because the forest is quite open. On the left was Fryingpan Creek and to the right and above, Goat Island Mountain. A peaceful forest, and I had the feeling that Indians of long ago wandered, maybe even camped in this area as they fished, hunted deer and elk, and gathered berries and herbs for food supply through the approaching winter. It must have been very untamed and hard during those centuries, struggling to survive the elements, bringing up babies, and probably always apprehensive of unfriendly strangers that may come onto them. The Native American's, as all cultures, have many social and external challenges to overcome. However, if people stay close to the earth and listen to the earth, I would say things would be clearer and easier. I hope some day that I may meet on a trail or ridge one of the *sensible* natives; perhaps have a talk of things now and of things that reach to the beginning and also of things maintained in a future.

As I hiked along I felt relaxed, energetic, the forest area projected clearness, calmness, an ease of thought. The natural environment has superior influence; it's been here a long time. Nature's knowledge is wise, experienced, it understands the origin of the planet. Walking along, I began to wonder what type of ethical principles a human might have toward these natural surrounds. There must be natural ethics. In many ways the human is an extension of nature, since human nature is part of nature. Near to where I stood was a large tree, it seemed a nice place to pause and rest, thus, I sat next to the tree and leaned against it – as I did I rubbed the back of my head on its bark. The fir towered high above its top most branches looked down to forest trees below. It was then that thoughts came of a natural responsibility, a human responsibility to the planet and all of nature. The world that we have occurred in is a world attached to our existence, and I wonder, what is the proper conduct necessary to share all here? I sat reflecting on this question and also on Native American's and other races of people born as they are on earth. I too looked to this country of the United States of America with its multitude and variety of nationalities, its citizens striving to engender a better life for family, friends, and self. I also viewed the Industrial Age, which exists in among various levels of society. All seemed quite vast when reaching into the thought of the different levels of a nation. 'Humanity has a natural responsibility to nature and that responsibility must be addressed,' but how and in what way? Sitting under the tall fir suddenly an impression came of an American Indian, a mental picture of his face, thought hovered within the impression; thought that went as follows, thought of what *he* had learned.

As I exist within this fluxing consciousness that I am—I will continue to walk and listen to the wind, hear and watch the birds, look to the clouds in sky, contemplate the moonlight and stars, feel the earth, and pass safely within and upon the water of stream.

I will heed the sound of the elk and deer, the hawk, and other flying creatures, the coyote and bear. I will observe the small animals and watch them in pursuit of what they do. I will appreciate them for only what they are, and respect them for what they are, and give them quarter if I can.

I will remember always to be selective in what I harvest – and what I do cut from nature – to show homage and give something in return, and not be wasteful of the life giving source that abides for all.

As I travel upon the land and smell the air with its message and feel the cold and rain and snow, I will also feel the warmth of sun and a glowing fire to warm me. In this I shall always remember not to abuse nature, or the animals, birds, and fish, for abuse is contrary to the living element – abuse is contrary to ones living existence.

These thoughts came swiftly and clearly, they continued and relayed more than I have recorded; the points in the last line sounded on in my mind, 'not to abuse nature—abuse is contrary to the living element.' It would be good to remember that point—again I rubbed the back of my head against the tall fir. Standing and running my hand over the moss-covered bark of that fir, it felt smooth in a rough sort of way. Glancing up its trunk toward the sky, this was an old tree, many centuries; it was growing before Columbus sailed to America, before America was even thought of or imagined as a nation – the sky above hidden from view, thick the trees upper canopy.

I walked on thinking of the natives that roamed here over the centuries, trying to envision a little glimpse of what it may have been like during a summer day such as the one I now experienced. Yet thoughts struggled within me as I tried to reach out, perhaps I wasn't considering how much there was to comprehend, thus, I reminded self of the vastness and measureless acumen or wisdom of nature, and that some things of awareness are not revealed quickly. That point I could accept as real, sort of a 'human necessity' I reasoned as I walked on—do leaders comprehend, does their knowledge range understand the elite natural essential that holds a Nation together?*

The location on the trail I had reached flattened on both sides of the path, the land quite level for a considerable distance except for a large mound of earth on my left toward the creek. I stopped and scanned that large pile of dirt which had many firs growing on it; somehow the mound seemed atypical, odd and unusual, placed amongst this level ground. I continued hiking not giving any further notice to it, then up ahead I saw another mound like the first one, this second mound was larger and tall, completely circular. It also was on the left toward the creek with large trees growing upon it. These mounds, one small the other large, both immediate and near each other. I surveyed the entire area thinking about landslides, for how did these gigantic mounds of earth get here and why were they perfectly round? As I've recorded, the surrounding area for a great distance in all directions was exceptionally level. I considered the mounds could be man-made, from another era, a history now lost to the chronicle of forgotten time. Level ground, perhaps a settlement area with mounds indicating a sacred site?

Hiking on I continued to think of this oddity within the forest near the creek and let my imagination wander upon the threshold of an unknown to see what may arise. Only speculative reflections came to mind. A burial ground, or perhaps a place of some type of gathering by those who lived here in another lapse of time. I knew it would take some convincing for me to agree that those dome shape mounds were from a natural occurrence. Imagery was realized as I walked. Sometimes poetical lines seem to inspire clearness as one learns to focus. The natural environment has clear energy the human can utilize to increase perception.

---

* President Teddy Roosevelt did understand and was aware, he acknowledged the essential—he comprehended it this way, quote, "We are not building this country of ours for a day. It is to last through the ages."

He was tall and slender
with night dark hair,
he stood and looked
to see me there,
he did not move
nor speak to me,
but he knew how good
this meeting seemed to be,
for now he had met someone who
might converse
at last in verse.

This all but seemed
filled with awe,
this shared glimpse
before the fall,
and in the light
that was so dim,
only thoughts
spoke within.

T'is very hard
to be sometimes,
quick and clear
with unknowns near,
for often when
we reach to them,
the things they bring
don't always sing,
and in the silence
of the mood,
reaction plays
and can be rude.

They were two
he and her,
she was short
petite and calm
with hair as soft
as duckling down.
Her gown was grey
weaved by day,
her feet were bare

and liked to play,
her hands did know
how to sow,
were strong and small and
could strike a blow.

They played at love
from dawn till dusk,
they swooned at noon
to see the moon,
when-ever came
the night of cold,
they held each other
within a fold.

They knew not how
to grant a wish,
but knew how too
catch the fish.

Together they climbed
high to sky
to watch the birds
as they did fly,
and in the time
when winter nears,
they went together
to chase the deer.
T'is then of cold
they found the old,
and came to rest
within a crest.

'The stream does flow
as does the snow,
the trees are dim
small light within,
we are at least
like feathers close,
to each other
more than most,
just her and I
in sweet refine,

reaching out
to our kind.'

'So when you climb
and pass the hill,
stop for a while
in forest still,

and if we can
send nature's boon,
when on your way
in light of day,
perhaps you'll find
a keepsake there –
know it was a gift we shared.'

Further along the way the trail came close to the creek, a place where solid rock is cut through, worn by the slicing force of water. The water roared over a narrow gape in the rock and plunged on down, moss grew here and there on its sheer face, deep green moss, a perilous view from where I stood looking to the waterfall. Gazing up-stream I could see a rocky area where big boulders lay—drawn there by that constant millstone known as gravity. Wide pathways existed like fingers where slides of snow and rock had opened and cleared within the exhaustive plunge of collapsing mountain. As I observed and traced the contoured clumps of boulders, sunlight seemed bright there and I felt as though I should climb up that gorge and explore. I didn't venture in that direction, perhaps another time.

Mountain willow and other green vegetation had sprouted everywhere clinging like tapestry within that steep mountain ravine; the various shades of green would be a challenge to capture with oil and brush. I felt a pull up to the ridge on high, inquiring sensations that were inquisitive yet formal; I sensed something looked down at me as I stood there on the trail feeling the hot August sun. The promontory I saw I took for Panhandle Gap, but it could have been an unnamed peak at 6798feet. Sarvent Glacier was somewhere in that area 2000feet up—further than what I probably could see from where I stood – I proceeded on through the forest.

A steep switchback was ahead, a climb where one could get their blood pumping, giving the body a workout. Several hikers passed, some women going up and some men coming down; we all seemed to meet near the zigzag area of the trail. Eventually the ambling path came out of the timber into an open valley where plants and tall shrubs had germinated and were plentiful. The path narrow and overgrown, sunlight brightly flashed in contrast to the shaded forest enclosure I just emerged from – the air hot and dry. Many tints of green flourished on up the valley and far in the distance tall mountain peaks were seen; there wasn't a breeze, today would be a scorcher.

The trail's location is on the south side of Goat Island Mountain. Goat Island Mountain at 7288feet is shaped like a round island, thus its name, and it also has mountain goats; the trail angles along amongst tall foliage everywhere. On the opposite side or perimeter of that circular mountain would be the White River campground, my hearth while I stayed in this area. The lofty region now opened with Fryingpan Creek streaming through it along with elk and deer tracks. Here vegetation increased. Further on, a small wood bridge, plus a wash crossing with large stones to foot across the stream. The options of the trail were plentiful, so it seemed as I hiked along, giving the hike variety, making it an enjoyable journey. Here one walks through an abundance of Hellebore (**VERATRUM VIRIDE**), the plant odor pungent – an aroma close to the ground – the fetor though mild, resembled the wet fir of elk or coyote. Further on another climb began, a steep switchback, the final approach to the meadow realm of Summer Land. Elk were here of recent for I saw fresh tracks on and off the trail. A park-sign was also posted ahead, carved on wood and quite weather worn that read, 'stay on switchback prevent erosion.' However, the elk had different ideas about climbing this mountain, and of course they didn't read signs, for I could see where they'd gone straight up through the switchback.

Beauty—about halfway up the switchback I saw her—she was still some distance away walking merrily along, ambling down the trail toward me; beauty is a young woman. She wore short shorts with an open white blouse and carried a daypack; reserved shapely warmth seemed to be strolling even frolicking in a kind of daydream. She was attractive, her blonde hair radiating desire and light, blue eyes clear, I stepped to the side of the trail to let her pass and nodded, she smiled but didn't stop to exchange pleasantries. Her perfume touched, it lingered—I gazed, her sensual walk and sway as she continued down the trail. Beauties smile—enticement alive, carnation scent and blush—illusion, or was it enchantment. That moment her daydream became my daydream, and I mused, *the mountain dream, could that be her*? Her perfume still drifting, wafting—her sweet smile lingering—in a blink, a mental picture appeared of the mountain dream in chapter one, was that her, the woman I dreamt of several days ago? Turning thoughts back to the hike, I looked up along the trail and again headed in that direction, however for a moment she still seemed there on the trail next to me—I had no choice but to let this momentary enchantment pass.

The meadows of Summer Land are rolling and small with alpine trees here and there; the soil was dry; a light color with short vegetation, there's a large rock shelter. Little Tahoma Peak seems near and Mount Rainier a little flatter. One can see Steamboat Prow and the Emmons Glacier laid in stillness upon the mountain. I looked northward slowly toward Goat Island Mountain, scanning its terrain, listening to instinct. There were a lot of open areas showing dirt and rock near its crown. Glassing those tracts with binoculars, they seemed alive – dancing with energy – near that area in a small group I glimpsed a band of elk bedded in the open. There were many brief meadows, plus I was surprised the elk were there this time of day in the open, for it was 12:30PM and hot. One large bull and a few cows were all that I could see, the distance long yet worth going to in sight; I wanted to be there in body too. Glancing to the SW—Meany Crest at 7973feet, shown along with what appeared to be Fryingpan Glacier. The glacial ice a light blue with a shade of turquoise, depending on how the light shown. The immediate surrounding rock ridges and slide areas reflected many color shades of stone; this locality has a variety of mineral compositions and deposits. Listening, I could hear off in the direction of Steamboat Prow (NW) a helicopter—focusing binoculars and searching that spot, I located the helicopter hovering near Camp Schurman, probably taking out garbage and dropping off supplies. Camp Schurman serves as base camp for climbers who ascend Mount Rainier from this side— permanent mountain rescue personal are there at all times during the summer season. They check to see that all climbers have proper permits and climbing gear, and of course are there in case of emergency. It was estimated that nearly 10,000climbers would try for the summit this year, ascending from many different routes, but I think because of the wet and cold weather the number will be greatly diminished. I was told that only about 50% of those that take on the challenge to reach Columbia Crest or Point Success, the very top of the mountain, succeed. Sometimes weather holds them back, also fatigue from high altitude sickness (something similar to seasickness), or any number of random occurrences could keep one from making the coveted zenith.

As I viewed the mountain with field glasses, the helicopter lifted off and flew low between Little Tahoma and Cathedral Rocks. It emerged through the binoculars about the size of a small dragonfly or even smaller; that view gave me a fine perspective of the dimension and proportion of this spectacular mountain. The massiveness of the glaciers, the crevices and rifts in the ice were extraordinary and larger than previously imagined. One begins to realize that Mount Rainier is surrounded by other mountain's and peaks – peaks above 8000feet— 14,411foot Mount Rainier is circled by mountains 8000-12,000feet—a mountain range in themselves. Looking high up toward the summit, using binoculars, I could see climbers like little black dots all in a row of four or more. Slowly they were ascending, some near the crown, some gathered in clusters, and some lower, I counted well over thirty. Like small miniature insects they seemed—I wondered if this calm and quiet immensity of nature would awaken someday as Mount St. Helens had more than a decade ago.

Putting the glasses back into my pack, I turned and walked to the shelter of Summer Land. The shelter is a haven from weather and very grand in size, its walls are made of large rock cemented together, the rafters of amply cut logs with a cedar shake roof that was new this year. A three sided shelter where one could easily bunk if the weather was harsh, wet, or snowing. The retreat's log rafters have also become a message-post—those beams are covered with many names, names in pencil, ink, and some carved in with a knife. Over the years many delighted and seasoned hikers have traveled this way to touch the mountain. They've arrived to scent the meadow, to breathe fresh air, to ski, to see what is here, and many also have left their mark in name and written word upon the silent sturdy shelter of Summer Land, I left mine there too.

Walking out of the shelter and along the trail toward a log nearby, its there I sat for lunch and relaxation. Summer Land is serene alive and pulsing, one feel's at ease – everything seems at rest; one is surrounded by many shades of green. I took out the bread I made at camp and laid it next to some cheese I'd already placed on the log. The camp bread is easy to make and tasty – here's the recipe. 2-cups flour, 1-cup water, 1 tablespoon baking powder, pinch of salt or sugar, mix the ingredients and flatten, add more flour if needed – the bread can be cooked on the hot coals of the fire wrapped in tinfoil or in a frying pan. It's called a 'damper'—Australian name. I'd fried mine in a large covered skillet with a lot of margarine, burned a little, but it still tasted good here in the high country.

The bread and cheese sliced thin and in small pieces I ate slowly, gazing off in the distance at the immense landscape before me, I marveled, the view of mountain seemed like a huge backdrop, a backdrop one might find on a stage of an opera. The mountain loomed behind and above the small alpine firs and meadow in forefront. Suddenly an aura of illusion appeared, I saw heat waves rippling and fluttering in the atmosphere with mountain in the background. The mountain appeared like a flickering projected hologram or electronic illusion, but I reminded myself that all was natural. Turning thoughts back to lunch, the cheese and bread were satisfying and as I ate I heard birds chirping somewhere in the trees, then a couple with backpacks walked by, 'nice looking twosome,' I mused, the young woman attractive, the young man filled with vigor showing rosy cheeks. Imagine the fun it would be doing the Wonderland Trail with a woman – how passionate the experience could be. A little while later another couple came along the trail, they were older, probably close to retirement age. The man had thin light hair and a smooth complexion, his wife short graying hair with a little darkness here and there. The man walked passed, but the woman stopped. I spoke commenting on how nice a day it was and how marvelous a place it seemed here in *the highlands*. She smiled and agreed as we carried on a casual conversation. She said her husband was a naturalist artist and that they hiked many places in the northwest to photograph settings for his oil paintings, and also to be in the out-of-doors. As we talked, her husband returned to where we both were and glanced at me as I slowly nibbled bread and cheese. Then his wife asked if I'd been in the shelter, I answered I had, and she added that former President John F. Kennedy had been here too, he had placed his name inside the shelter along with all the others. She insisted I go with her and see his signature, so I put down the bread and cheese and followed while her husband looked on toward the mountain. We walked the short distance to the shelter then entered, and there near the back on the right she pointed to a rafter, there written in pencil, 'John F. Kennedy, Mass. August 1947'. She said she had found it when they had visited here in the late 1970's. We both looked at the words and noticed that someone had traced over his name in pencil so it would be more readable. She commented that the tracing denoted or may exhibit a question of authenticity. Neither of us carried that part of our conversation to the point of exact clarity, leaving it to the annual of truth. I felt it was authentic and knew she did too, and I asked her if she had put her name here, she said she hadn't. We strolled out together, and as we did she commented that it was too bad what happened to him (JFK) and I nodded in concordance and remarked that it was a shame that one of our Presidents would have died that way. She agreed speaking in a soft and tender tone of voice; the lady was a gentlewoman. When we reached her husband they both said goodbye and went upon their way.

I again sat on the log and looked to finish my bread and cheese, but it wasn't there, the chipmunks and birds had stolen it, the critters up there are very hungry and I'm sure one or several of them really gorged themselves on my 'damper' and cheese. Reaching into my pack, I pulled out a record book and jotted down some notes, a few descriptions that I thought important to remember of this hike to Summer Land. Then standing and stowing everything, I threw my small pack over my shoulder and headed on down the trail toward Fryingpan Creek. Before I had reached the switchback I saw a middle age man hiking up, he stopped to take photographs. That location on the trail was a place where one was pressed by the full impact of the mountain in the distance—the summit seemed to sing with orchestration. Mount Rainier from where I stood came alive and sang to me in a silent way, wafted melodiously through the airy, but how? The sensation was a kind of melodic harmony, a tonal wave similar to symphony. I instantly imagined an open-air stage with conductor and all; high notes of string and wind instruments reverberating in tones harmonious, soothing, and penetrating. That's how it seemed as I let imagination free to pursue that essence of thought, thought envisioning a huge audience in attendance seated on a massive mountainside amphitheater. Carrying the inspiration further, I pictured Chopin or Mozart, Verdi or Stravinsky, all part of a large midsummer performance, their hands and fingers in unison as they moved them along the piano keyboard playing in symphonic harmony. Perhaps on just such a sunny afternoon in August somewhere in a once removed distant mountain kingdom or realm, such a performance was taking place; the emotion was great as too the thought of attending such a performance. If only we could look into the world of Divine Arrangement, perhaps such a view would help us truly know and understand the way of the heart. I smiled and acknowledged the full grace that these Summer Land surroundings inspired. Glancing to the mountain in bright sunlight, then to the shaded ground and up again to the mountain, the sudden exhilaration-infusion of brightness which came from the white snow and massive shape of the summit of Mount Rainier seemed to sing through to the silent meadow of my mind. And again I was able to behold another motif for the word and emotion of Awesome.

Continuing my walk along the trail, I neared the photographer and stopped to tell him about the elk that were across the valley and up on top of Goat Island Mountain. He became excited at the news and headed hurriedly for a better vantage point to see them as they lay bedded in the bright and hot sun of summer that we were experiencing after a cold and wet July. Resuming my walk down the dirt trail, I began to whistle 'Waltzing Matilda' – a tune that has always seemed dear to me. The pace was fast now, all descending, I moved with ease, feeling the wind on my face, smelling the Hellebore, hearing the bees, viewing the many color tints of flora and feeling the heat on my lips and tongue from the hot air of the day. At the little wooden bridge I passed the naturalist painter and his wife, but didn't stop, I wanted to keep my stride going. Inside of self there was a great joy of some sort, as though I was closer to a part within, a part that I had always wanted to meet. Moving faster, almost wanting to run, the combination of momentum and elation I felt seemed to build. It was a good deep feeling that one may have as they soared within the fervent and passionate realm of unrestricted familiarity. A complete spontaneous uninhibited sensation that was natural and free floating on high with today's breeze. Somewhere near the edge of where the tall trees begin to align with surrounding openness, I slowed to my normal walk it was then that I saw on the trail a large feather. I stopped, picked it up and smoothed it with my fingers. The feather was white with gray, light brown on the edges, the gray tint very slight in its silver-white cobalt hue. I recognized it to be that of a Goshawk (**ACCIPITER GENTILLIS**) and I stuck it in my hat. It must have fallen there since the time I had gone up, for it was in a location on the path that one couldn't miss seeing as they passed. I was pleased with this find, a gift from nature, and I accepted the feathered fineness without reservation. That plume is now added to my collection of memorabilia, items of the wilderness—I feel as though a part of Summer Land and Mount Rainier have come home with me within the presence of the feather. It was 2:32PM when I reached the truck and headed back to the White River campground where I would wash and take a nap during the heat of this day.

It always seems so new
when I visit you,
and as the time goes by
I clearly find within my mind
simple things combined,
with complex riddles too
that seem to fit so nice
to all the things I do,
that as I hike your trails,
and view the mountain too,

I cannot help
but really know,
I'm in love with you.

Mount Rainier 1993

Tipsoo Lake ∆∆∆∆∆

Evening reached for coolness of twilight—slanting rays of sun caressed with shadowy glows in peaceful waves of stillness. Serene melodious sensation fluttered with drift and hover. Tantalizing alluring notions danced to an emotional pulse like Eleusinian performers surrounded with muse and mystery, intoxicating ambience, shaping to form mood and temperament, swirling, spinning, and warming. Soft invisible spectrum rays of filtering color light came as soothe through the trees, a whisper to satisfy thoughts of contentment and pleasure. Sunset, rushing forth embracing, assimilating, integrating and inducing with passion this summer nights approach. Birds scurried about looking for a last small bit of nourishment to take them through the night, chirping, hopping, moving quickly here and there, head and eyes turning, glancing, peering in all directions. Unique creatures with feathers soft in fluff, feet scaled like reptilia, woven for protection as armor with claws to *grip* the roost or hold a morsel of food for sharp beak to pluck and rip. Small keen eyes, miniature magnifiers, exceptional telescopic eye's for the large high fliers, eyes to direct a moment pecking for seed and insect. Each bird in solo singing its own individual song, all singing together with symphonic harmony; perceptive the infinite mind and being that connected the plausible, logical, believable bond to create feathered friend—bird.

Sitting next to the campfire at the White River campground at 4400feet, dinner was over and I felt energetic as this nighttime approach infused me with its magical delight. Sky clear, the air fresh, mountain air is different than city air—as I relaxed I knew it was time to gather a summery together of my stay at Mount Rainier. The character, surroundings, and experience of this visit were blending to form a dimensional realm, a sphere like world; a metaphysical domain that my identity and perception had created from the multitude of places, views, sounds, colors, touches, tastes, and angles of thought. As I sat, I envisioned emotion and passion walking arm in arm with realism and inspiration, that foursome strolling together within the calm moments of evening. From that imagined path like realm of combine, new awareness magically emerged manifesting-materializing, indicating yet a next level of awareness and understanding to reach; I hoped to find pleasing new experiences there, a consent of my own making. Tonight the moon would be full, a blue moon this night would bring. I thought about the moon's arrival near midnight and also how long it would be until another blue moon would align in calculated formation. Yes, rare is a visit of blue moon*.

Dimensional spheres, metaphysical openings, mountain of awe, moonlight dreams, pink glowing mountainous sunrises, hovering halo summit cloud, watery taste sweet, white-silver plume a feather gift, passionate and emotional sensation, provocative seductive inspiration, imagined invisible doorways created to hold thought and reality together, and alas—distinctive blue moon. I pondered these reflections, a woven weave of mind placed as momentary impressions knitted in a sweater design to create warmth for body, heart, and mind; generating longevity realization. Heaven and Earth, pendulum swing, illusions of the fleeting kind with depicting seasons, opposing months and varying landscapes, sun moon stars—phenomenon's, nighttime ecliptic refraction's, aurora borealis, lightning and rainbows, thunder—expressions earth. These also were a woven weave of a

---

*Blue moon, the origin of this expression often is used to mean *a rare event*; it also suggests a reference to the second occurrence of a new Moon in one calendar month—another consideration is that atmospheric effects occasionally give the Moon the color appearance of blue.

kind established presented on earth, natures endeavor to open a lane, to create focus, a path, a trail for a pilgrimage to begin, a pilgrimage through mountainous ways. As I sat next to the fire with coals aglow an image of the white staircase, that dream flashed through my mind, a vividly clear image, yet, I knew that special stair was a stairway most difficult to find. I sipped from the cup of tea that I held in my hand and it tasted good. Suddenly there was a great urge to take a drive in the slanting shades and tranquil soft glows of eventide. The campfire embers were twinkling out, setting the cup down I stood from the picnic table and walked to the truck. Driving along the lane I stopped at Mattie's campsite, thinking she might like to join me. Mattie was a woman that I'd met a year ago while camping. Slender, warm and pleasant, medium height, gentle sensitive features, energetic, yet vulnerable she appeared to me in many ways. Mattie had shielded her innocent naïveté and childlike self with a cloak of durable sternness and reserved control. However, I had learned to look through that exterior veil, a point I never mentioned to her, and saw there within her clear eyes a woman who I could only admire and feel deeply toward. Friends, she wished us to be, and I accepted for that too was part of her veil. Stopping the truck at her campsite, I stepped out and walked to her picnic table where she stood, and asked, "want to take a drive…have a look around?" She smiled and answered that she would, so the two of us got in the truck and drove down the road. "Where to tonight," she asked. "How does Tipsoo Lake sound, up on Chinook Pass," I answered glancing toward her. "Ah, the lake," she responded, "it's very nice, I like it there." We both in our singular and separate ways endeavored to be free to roam at will within the grand essay of life, unbridled, unconstrained, as we reached to touch and behold the environment, habitat, the atmosphere of which we live. We had shared many good times hiking, exploring, and observing nature's wilderness with its natural essentials and all else it entailed. In many ways we helped each other become more aware of our surroundings and inner selves. Sharing too help and helping to share. I didn't do well in the 'helping the other share' category, for I was caught up in writing and my other pursuits. A truth I can clearly acknowledge, hopefully at some future time and place I'll learn to know and live the 'helping the other share' component, which is so necessary.

Truth is a path that leads to everything of use to us—when one strays from truths path, only dead ends appear—the human must strive to be free of encased domination and untruths. One must acknowledge that all humans are of equal value. Though some may not contribute equally, still their human value is there. It's the total composite—humanity has a valuable capacity, a compatible linkage to everything in this world of which it exists. An example, the capacity composite I'm focusing on may be expressed this way. Look to the night sky and there see the great river of all rivers—Milky Way Galaxy—see how it shines, sparkles, twinkles in the heavens. That great river sends its visual glow to enliven and silently speak to our mind, to convey a subconscious message, cosmic beam Milky Way. Innumerable radiance Milky Way, vastness preserved within a multitude of visual awe—cluster formations, constellations, stars, individual singularity sublime the Milky Way. Each emitting light equal in value to all other light's for together they comprise a total, each sparkling light equally necessary for the entirety. Neither is one light dominant over another—all lights are working in unison toward a greater glow.

Dominating untruths are like veils, dark-age blocks, obstacles, impediments of restraint, they must be realized and avoided—one knows it's not wise for the eyes to deceive, nor is it advisable to be deceived by a hidden deception. As we visit the natural world and view how uniquely it performs, we absorb its actuality as a tangible fact. That natural actuality acknowledgement is perceptiveness; it becomes strengthened because we've absorbed the natural truth energy. A firm foundation is then formed, a foundation that establishes new awareness; imbalances diminish. When clear renewal takes place we become refreshed, obstacles and impediments become removed, individuality opening enhancing reinforcing as one moves onward. Learn how to 'let go'; letting go of old thinking is not easy, however, if one is to grow beyond a negative hold, letting go must be done. The world of nature creates 'new thinking' to replace old thinking.

The night air was calm and warm but up at the lake it would be cool, especially after sunset. As we cruised from camp we crossed the main bridge of the White River, unique in design that bridge, very stout and solid in appearance. Its material consists of large rock, chiseled and chipped to give a rugged surface texture. Honed decades ago, it was built by a group of Austrian stonemasons; their European design expresses an original style and personality, the European Alp's. Secure, firm, substantial in composition, hardy, stalwart, and stable in strength—a bridge built to last. Further along the road were a series of small bridges with similar design where streams and brooks rush and pour forth from off steep forest heights.

The stone bridges along that stretch of road instill visual harmony a merge with landscape, a visitor seems to ride through earthy pastures which don't have the metal, concrete, and wire rope of an Industrial Age.

Several miles further we turned right onto highway [410], also named the Mather Memorial Parkway, and headed toward the passes. There are two here, the first is Cayuse Pass at 4694 feet, then Tipsoo Lake, and a little beyond, Chinook Pass at 5432 feet. Chinook Creek springs out of Tipsoo Lake down to where it meets the Ohanapecosh (O·hana·pe·cosh) River. The Chinook runs south, the Ohanapecosh River, south-southeast. There are many waterfalls in this area but they may be hard to get too because it's rocky and steep – a rough terrain; rock climbers may find this region gripping if they're the exploring and inquisitive type. Naches Peak and Yakima Peak are laid on a line east and west; Tipsoo Lake and Chinook Pass nestled between. Yakima Peak I estimate to be near 6300 feet, its west of Naches Peak (also estimated) near 6500feet. These two peaks have meadows that slope mildly up to them along with many trails; a picnic area is at Tipsoo Lake. Just over Chinook Pass one will find a large parking area and facilities for a common human requirement we all maintain. The Pacific Crest Trail* meets at Chinook Pass as it ranges through the mountainous wilderness of the Pacific Northwest. The way to Chinook Pass from the western side climbs as a large switchback, a moderate grade built on the side of lofty promontories, it's usually closed during winter due to snow. As we drove and glanced down to the right, the valley below was dark and swept to the south toward the area of Mount Adams and Mount St. Helens. At another bend of the road the view stretched north along Klickitat (Klic·ki·tat) Creek, which descends to the White River below.

Tipsoo Lake was calm with lacquer like sheen when we arrived. Dispersed light reflected off its smooth surface – surrounding peaks radiating a serene transparent-azure, tempered light of sky. Translucent blue sapphire tint everywhere did blend with dark watery lake and background greens. 'Mystical atmosphere,' I mused, 'a realistic and natural presentation.' As Mattie and I

---

*The Pacific Crest Trail covers 2500miles from Mexico to Canada, takes at least 5 months to complete, 6 months would be more reasonable. Starting in April, 3Months through California at 1600miles, 3months for Oregon and Washington; the Washington to Canada trek would have to be completed by the end of September; weather becomes rough in October with high elevation snowstorms.

strolled we saw the moon reflected on the mirror plane of Tipsoo—I glanced upward to see the moon's twilight opal-blush. The unescorted and solitary moon rose slowly pale and bright and seemed to be glancing toward soft golden sun, which slowly settled into the distant western horizon as ecliptic shadowy shade of darkness night approached.

We walked along the path near the shore glimpsing sudden riffles from a soft breeze that skipped across adaptable flexible medium—water. In soothing sway zephyrs' caressed the watery smooth as though with a spirit conception touch—surrounding quietude. Little fish jumped here and there sending circular riffles outward, showing quintessence and rolling motion. Flies and insects flew over the water, anxious, enthusiastic, and almost impatient as calm evening twilight color imbued all nearby. The air fresh and scented by the encompassing fragrance of an adjoining meadow, its surrounding prudent green and colorful flora served to enclose and cradle the small lake. Birds flew and hopped about chirping singing speaking, melodious songlines true. Stationary lake and untroubled meadow did lay-prevail upon this dwelling place high up near the sky. A site where one felt peace and quietness soothe—childlike waves of innocence. At that moment a silent calm existed which opened toward feelings, an expression similar to what one may experience while viewing a sleeping child just before it awakens. I vividly saw in mind just such a child—the child opened its eyes, peered directly at me, an instant awakening—childlike waves of innocence sprung forth from peaceful slumber—envisioned just so was Tipsoo Lake; newness had awakened.

Mattie and I sat on a log bench near the water on the eastside of the lake and looked westward. The fish of the lake still leaped everywhere creating little isolated circular patches of riffle. The riffles were immured like miniature island riffle-collages that pulsed and changed with each passing moment, moment's that seemed to transcend to another time. A time and place separate, once removed—as imagination might be—yet still possessing rational action and passionate thought. An animistic reality had occurred, for delight, enchantment and enlightenment were present – so flared Tipsoo Lake. Body and mind surrounded with deep stillness like moon and lake, gentle surrounds. All was at rest, embodiment in cadence as physical and mental embraced each other—corporeal spirit that domain of self was alert and teeming with the cause of evening. "It's very beautiful here, at peace," I said to her who sat next to me, a woman with soft blue gray eyes. She didn't reply, for she too must have been experiencing an encounter, rendezvous, appointment, privately her own. I let self fuse with this freedom of harmony and the accord I felt was one of wholeness and unity. I affirmed this moment was a connecting intersection, a converge merge waiting to be established and instilled as an opening for something new and fresh. I reasoned that I would have this newness, for it was generous, kind, reliable, and not oppressive. I looked up to the blue twilight sky, an unlimited sky where eyesight and perception were free to roam at will, clear and cloudless the sky with its boundless extending vastness. Emotion and passion rushed in my blood, sensation natural and good. I was at peace with the world and self, and this newness I yielded too freely letting it flourish and join to become part of my total existence.

After a while we rose from our log seat near shore of lake and walked to the truck – senses alert and fixed in permanent sway – memory now possessed these surrounds to replay and manifest somewhere, someplace, at another time. Mountainous ways filter through the confines of the human heart to kindle a flame, to bring new light, and instill the heart with a nerve of awe, the sense of awesome. A mountains presence ignites wholeness as it shares hidden fire – a fire that travels along our pathway of perception enlivening the awareness of what we really are and may really be. Given freely, spontaneously, mountainous ways levitate a lofty completeness. In many ways the mountain expresses *a great sharing*. 'There's something magical even mystical about Tipsoo Lake,' I mused, as we drove away and up over Chinook Pass.

Down the other side of the pass one finds a large parking lot where they can stop for a while. There were many visitors at the rest area, young couples walking hand in hand, parents and children laughing and exchanging momentary thoughts and recognition as mountainous ways reached them too. Elderly couples and singles taking pictures—some just standing in matured silence letting their past tumble and whirl into the immediate. I saw people of all races at this rest station; an International juncture of leisure placed on high. Glancing to the ridge surrounding me and then toward the distant eastern skyline – I knew this evening would always be remembered, a time and place, a special dominion within 'the summer of a blue moon'. Continuing to gaze east down the wide valley, a broad expansive valley that extends far, I saw the Rainier Fork that flows into the American River, tributaries pouring eastward. Above to the west was Yakima Peak steep and rocky with an antenna planted firmly and sticking up like a beacon of some sort. Another reminder of the technical world we live in, but I knew someday antennas such as that would not be necessary. Leaving the parking area we returned up the pass and glancing out the window of the truck—there high in the sky we saw two hawks gliding on surges of warm air, we stopped to view them.

Hawk gliding high
the air,
drifting to motion
the wind,
gaining altitude
to dive,
searching for food
enjoying the mood,
seeing all to see
feeling so keen – Hawk
knowing how to be.

Hawk with features
brown and dark,
wings out stretched
to reach a mark,
tail moves sideways
up and down,
a rudder wind
above the ground.

Hawk by two
they did fly,
over head
what could be said,
we watched them
long,
they watched us
too,
both aware
was time to roost.

The day was ending
with rising moon,
the sun was setting
not all to soon,
the air was cool
refreshing still,
the lake in peace
now knew us well –
reflecting too
its loving spell.

Continuing, we drove over the pass and down the other side, stopping again near the Tipsoo Lake picnic area. Across the highway is an open field of alpine forest and meadow. Grazing on the lush green vegetation that grew upon those meadows were a small band of elk. One large bull and two lesser bulls with about half a dozen cows; I felt there were more elk in the surrounding timber. The large bull grazed, but now and then would look up to keep his eye on the other bulls. It would not be long and they would be in the 'rut', breeding time, and these bulls would become very aggressive, mean, and unpredictable. The muscles of the large bull were massive, his hair light color and thick, however, his antlers were medium size, which made his body appear even larger. The cows moved slowly and paid little attention to the bulls, they seemed unimpressed with the presence of them.

After a while we continued down the road from Tipsoo Lake toward camp and as we did I asked Mattie if she'd like to have a cup of coffee in Packwood, the first town along the road south, about 20miles away. She smiled and said she would, there was still a lot of light in the sky.

Mount St. Helens ΔΔΔΔΔΔ

The next few days following the visit to Tipsoo Lake were spent relaxing at camp and writing, typing a rough draft of the events and experiences up to that point. Trying to express the mood and feel of the mountain isn't easy; the metaphorical personification of nature is challenging, its metamorphic invisibleness difficult to describe. I find it necessary to record many idea themes while in the field, in the field one often finds a line of thought quite different to those found while in the comfort of home. Sometimes the simplest expression found under a tree is an expression to trigger a vast and expressive theme. There seems to be a clear inspiration present when writing in the field, the energy is different compared to city environment—it's almost as though the city is encased within some sort of enclosure separate to what one finds in the wilderness. There are a lot of positive points to writing in the field.

After finishing the first draft of this visit to Mount Rainier, Mattie and I decided to leave the area for a day and drive south to Mount St. Helens. It was September 2nd—the weatherman forecasted clear skies and hot temperatures. Mattie was excited and so was I, for neither of us had ever visited that National Volcanic Monument of which we both had heard so much. We wore our shorts and took along a little lunch, sunglasses, camera, binoculars, and a jug of water. The Dodge ran smoothly up over Cayuse Pass where we turned onto highway [123] that would take us out of the park just passed the Ohanapecosh campground. From there we headed toward Packwood on highway [12] and to the small city of Randle where we would turn left onto route [25], which went to Mount St. Helens National Park.

The land near and around Randle is flat, a wide valley with many farms and large open stretches of pasture, also it's an area where several ranches raise and breed horses. The Cowlitz River streams through this meadow valley; as we drove west, the scent of cut hay from surrounding fields floated in the air, fields whose color had faded from lush green to a dry grass tone. That shade of decline, dead grass and vegetation, falling leaf's, reflects clearly an ominous allusion that indicates frosty mornings as winter approached. I never preferred autumn, of course for many it's a nice time of year, however, it's to exact in extinct character for me to accept. The thought of extinction along with things perishing, fading – the ebb of life is not something that I find very desirable. The seasonal change that occurs with foliage falling, birds leaving, plants dead, trees standing naked numb and spent is not my cup of tea. The sinister and foreboding shades of autumn have always felt apprehensive, as though an impending apocalyptic storm approached—autumn—a deep omniscient message. A yearly message reminder to all, that a provoking force is present within each and every *autumn notice*; an imminent impending notice. Autumn's emissary displayed at first in beautiful sprays of color to dazzle mind and emotion are in reality a sweet-sour type of expression. For on the one hand the colors are spectacular, yet on the other, once the color is gone what do we see – just a lot of dead leaf's and barren trees. Autumn's emissary is not really one I find pleasing—such an envoy I imagine only as a herald of Omen. A cryptic forewarning *that* courier, an intuition link and message of a kind, a subtle message hint for the subconscious indicating autumn's dormancy is present. Are there any other ways to view the character of autumn? Are there other ways and directions in which mankind may look, or may-not-be looking, or should be looking? There seems a great imbalance present and expressed in many forms, one example; we're taught that we live in a kind of out-of-reach world that has many impossibilities.

Impossibility conditioning is a mode we have been schooled to accept – a mode that actually conflicts with ones longevity pattern. Impossibility thinking—a pattern a society can be locked too and controlled by; such a dilemma is held in place by leader's who are impossibility minded. Another example is, even though it may seem impossible to hold autumn off, still one may wonder if autumn could shorten or summer lengthen? We have seen the human life span lengthen, and some scientists have hinted that the human body should function longer than it does presently. On many social levels ones life is linked to impossibility. One must realize such an impossibility mindset can be dissolved and replaced with a form of 'it is possible' as in living longer.

It is clear in my thinking that a great imbalance has occurred on this planet – much has happened in the 7000years leading up to now. The *imbalance* has far reaching consequences and effects that reach into the entire solar system. The imbalance is a concept-direction one can look toward and be free of with mild difficulty; beware of 'phase controls'. Phase-controls bring nothing but havoc and a multitude of chaotic forms—destruction and extinction. Perhaps that's what imbalance is, merely a troublesome phase control.

As we drove along I began to wonder how Mount St. Helens would be in comparison to the form-theme of autumn and winter, would it be desolate, bleak, and windswept. As we turned left onto route [25], Mattie indicated the information center of Mount St. Helens would be along the road. The Woods Creek information center was our first exposure to Mount St. Helens and what lay ahead. There were books, pictures, videotapes, maps, and a nice woman attendant that gave us an interpretive map marked to show sites to see. In a few minutes we again were on our way.

The paved road curls and climbs with only a few straight stretches. Eventually we passed Iron Creek, and at Wakepish Sno Park turned onto [99] which would take us to Windy Ridge, the end of the road where one has an excellent view of the volcano, plus, at Windy Ridge there were interpretive talks on Mount St. Helens eruption. As we cruised along we saw tall and beautiful timber, lush green foliage, huckleberry shrubs, many birds, and also flowers that lined the road; the air heating up, yet there were cool shaded areas here and there. The road we followed was dreamy like country roads of old one often sees on film where all seems calm, peaceful, no harshness. Sort of like imagining a visit to grandma and grandpa; folks with a small farm or cottage nestled away somewhere in the country. Mattie and I were filled with anticipation as we ambled along, expectations building as we approached the natural phenomenon of Mount St. Helens. Pictures or films have difficulty capturing an event or region the way visiting does, a point we both learned during our own travels over the years.

Within my thought of erupting volcano's I imagined such things as St. Elmo's fire, that corposant ball of light that can float, whirl, twirl, and spin as its light beam is drawn to the bosom of earth. Driving along in silence, I wondered and questioned, even attempted to theorize what may have been deep in Mount St. Helen's to cause the eruption. What sparked such eruptive power to ignite; I found no answer as I closed the thought, only theories, however, there must be someone somewhere that knows the truth of it all.

As we gained altitude, the surrounding vegetation began to thin, and suddenly, instantly—all vegetation ended, a total stop—we had reached the devastation zone. Bear Meadow is that first viewpoint, the frontline. Beyond here was a place one saw as no-man's land, everything resembled the look of a giant battlefield. We were still over 10miles away and could not see the mountain, but the devastation, the undoing, had reached this far. Looking down into a valley that extended for miles, probably the Clearwater area, there was nothing but a terrain similar to what one may find on a desert, totally barren ground, only rocks and ridges. The desolation present was greater than any forest fire region one may see. The scale of destruction extended without interval—nothing seemed to impede, halt, or hide from the force released that day of the eruption.

We parked, stepped out of the truck at a viewpoint and looked eastward—in the distance we saw Mount Adams at 12,307feet, all snow covered and majestic. As I looked at Mattie and the surrounding barren terrain, and then to Mount Adams, I felt a strong and silent expression of remorse radiating in a multitude of ways, and with that remorse a clear sense of regret. The comparison between Mount Adams in the distance and the now Mount St. Helen's area in front of us was truly paradoxical, a paradoxical illustration. It was hard to believe that the terrain where I now stood was a short time ago the same as the view of Mount Adams. What I saw as the result of the eruption were inconsistent landscapes, contradictory dissenting and opposing landscapes, disagreeable in nature—a defined contrast now existed between the two mountains. To me, that was totally paradoxical. As one looked to Mount Adams, it would be contradictory to suggest such devastation could occur, but where I stood was the stark reality that such destruction can occur— thus the paradox had substance. I now realized a paradox could also carry an emotion of regret—an emotional form attached to a past. To overcome regret one must look to a positive future. But can one have such a future without paradoxical attachments of destruction? I felt such a future was possible but not easily attainable in a world where destructive mindsets and leaders exist.

We moved on up the road, the sun bright and hot, there wasn't any shade, the wind dry; everything seen was a critical-zone; pensive and serious. Soon on the right we reached the Meta Lake Miner's Car all rusted and smashed, the roof crushed in; the car seemed sterile and weightless within its shrouded guise, a car seen by all as they passed this way. We didn't stop to have a close look at the car; it was more than our emotion wanted to take in at this time, the family who owned the car 'were taken' that day of the eruption. Suddenly I felt much sorrow; I don't know if the sadness was from what happened to the family or from those that were now here, or simply a reflection of my own. I believe there is much to understand about sorrow. Sorrow in many ways is difficult to accept or understand and I feel *that* part of our persona is easier to acknowledge when one is with someone who is close, or with a friend who will share the emotion felt at the time. For with sharing, people can gather helping strength, which is natural and pinnacle to their understanding of sorrow and all it represents or conveys.

Next we came to Independence Pass where one sees Spirit Lake below and the thousands of broken splintered trees that float on its surface. Looking down at the lake, I thought I saw sailboats fluttering in the wind, but when I searched there with binoculars, what appeared at first to be sailing craft turned out to be small white clumps of earth that pointed up out of the ruffled water of the lake. The scene was a curious thing—and one may wonder that perhaps in a distant future sailboats ride the waves, embrace the wind, and kiss the water as they sail upon the breezy clean surface of that Spirit Lake. We drove from Independence Pass up to Cedar Creek and as we approached I asked Mattie if we should stop. She said to drive on too Windy Ridge, that the devastation, destruction and ruin, were 'a little much'. For as far as one could see all was stark, bereft, and wanting. One sensed, felt a deep penetrating silence, anguish almost mournful. I tried to define those low tones and had great difficulty in doing so. It seemed we were in a vast void with fear and immense lack, tremendous need. Something within my human nature trembled, quivered, and shivered.

Surroundings radiated agony and distress that the inner-self consciously wanted to block. The muffled intonation that I felt, I couldn't define – no words came as we drove along. The unfaltering pressure emerged and filtered through me, it seemed to reach far into the principality of soul. As it did, I realized the positive self was calling and needed to be recognized. Thus, I began to look for the affirmative, the constructive and beneficial spirit that resided here; an assenting form. I saw small huckleberry's sprouting, alders, many small plants, some flowers, large reforestation areas with young firs' waist high, birds flying in sky—instantly the deep foreboding tension vanished. The earth with its imperishable constant was rebuilding Mount St. Helens. The matron of nature was here, present and residing, engaging to heal this ailing and yearning landscape. I felt a great hope with promise, trust, and desire. It's important one recognizes and understands the need to think, speak, and act in the affirmative. In positive thought and action a natural reality exists – is present to be acknowledged. That authentic presence, and ones pilgrimage toward its positive awareness, helps one rise to a site where they can behold a truer reality; genuine understanding.

Mattie and I parked at Windy Ridge and walked to the open-air interpretive center where the program was beginning. The view of Mount St. Helens is near, immediate. One sees what remains of the mountain after the eruption; the open cavity, crater, and devastation is extraordinary. A woman speaker presented a description of what took place.

In March of 1980, earthquakes began and continued for weeks and during that time a bulge began to grow on the side of the mountain. In May on the day of the eruption there was an earthquake that measured 5.0 in magnitude. That tremor fractured the large protruding bulge on the side of the mountain sending it down to Spirit Lake. The bulge was thrust forward by the shock of the earthquake and that released pressure below, thus, a tremendous explosion occurred. The force that came from that explosion is said to have created a shockwave 24miles wide; that wave traveled 200mph and built in momentum to a maximum of 600mph, the blast wave was felt 17miles away. Everything in the immediate area of the shock-wave path was blown over – all the forest was laid down in one great push. The timber around Spirit Lake was blown to the ground then the side of the mountain slid into the lake. The force from that giant landslide sent the water of the lake rushing toward its far end, of course the squall from the explosion had already blown down the forest and as that wall of water reached the far hills it traveled 800feet up. Then the water rushed back bringing with it many blown down trees, those are the ones seen floating in the lake today. The snow and ice and summit of Mount St. Helens followed down behind the blast and bulge, what remains of the summit can be seen across the way from Windy Ridge. The homes, dwellings on the lake, and everything prior to this eruption are now buried 210feet under the rubble that slid down the mountain that eventful day.

The woman that gave the interpretive talk explained all in one of the best, if not the best, interpretative narrative that I've attended. She also spoke of feeling the earth, of listening and rejoicing in the revitalization of the earth at Mount St. Helens. She reflected that new vegetation was appearing, that birds, animals, and fish were starting anew. That the eruption though harsh and deadly (57-dead or missing) was over, a new day had begun with replenishing growth to replace all that had vanished. I was impressed with everything the talented woman had said, I'm sure the 50 or so other visitors there were equally impressed. After the program, Mattie and I walked back to the truck and had lunch, took pictures; it was windy and after a while we headed back to Mount Rainier. On our way down from this mountain we noticed more new growth and were amazed at how quickly the earth can began to recover – thirteen years after the fact.

It seemed good to return to Mount Rainier and camp. In a few days I would be leaving the mountain, returning to the peninsula, city, apartment, and my abode in the Pacific Northwest. However, I knew something would be going with me, something that now was permanently linked and imprinted upon the total I am. For mountainous ways and the mountain had placed their gift of impression, love, passion, and personality, firmly within me. I knew as I traveled on, that wherever my life may lead I would always have and remember Mount Rainier's vivid moonlit nights where dreams abide, the daylight hikes where reality surrounds, and the snowy even sensuous view of lofty heights.

Alexander Volenski

A Poem △△△△△△△

Now it comes
to other things,
for it is time to walk again
in another place,
within another wind,
to listen too the sounds
that all abound,
as my feet step by step
move me along.

And *there on high*
she touched me so,
here below
on earth I go,
and in my mind
I'll always know,
she's there somewhere
a place so fair.

Perhaps some day
yet to come,
there will be a place
where we can sun,
and warm our hearts
to our content,
recalling all
that love had sent.

Surrounding hills
in seasoned light,
surging streams
beyond my sight,
flying birds with feathered wing,
I'll see as you
while songs they sing.

And in the night
when stars shine bright,
and moon above
shows haloes white,
I'll think of you

with fond delight,
and hope someday
to be again
with you there
in starlight fair.

Natures verse abounds in place,
smooth and light
like waters bright,
natures verse does roll sometime,
like meadow hills
of summer sights,
natures verse abrupt and slow,
is a verse
we learn to nurse,
for as we go
upon the ridge,
rocky steep and jagged there,
so too we move
in stops and starts,
listening too
our beating heart –
the verse up there
like down here,
we know in fact
has no real lack,
for as we read
that rugged verse,
we see in mind
and are alert,
for on the high
and pinnacle peak,
we walk a trail
abrupt jagged craggy and rough,
sight is keen
rides aloft,
as on the air
where clouds do flair.

So as one reads
within the verse,

they listen look
within themselves –
more than when
they read the news –
for here one finds
themselves a truth.

From spirit dream
to *halo cloud*,
a walk in forest
a talk to self,
tiny bird sipping so,
flowers grow so very low,
heightened trail
a meadow land,
a place of rest
where man can stand,
as little pond flows on down.

Mountains near
air very clear,
whitened peaks
sober there,
snow-like hair
a lady fair,
waters stream
the inter fork,
people laugh
they are so young,
filled with vigor
handsome comely too,
jolly they sit
below summits' hue,
a quest they share
high in the air.

There upon a rock I lay
under the sun above,
catching rays
thinking love,
thunder comes
from high above,
is it Jupiter – Mars

a herald too –
and as I swoon
recalling moon,
feeling warmth
from sun so hot,
cheerful happy
mirthful too,
the full grown
men and women move,
pass by me
they're filled with glee,
I open eyes
move feet to go
on down the trail
to camp I know.

Oh *summer land*
wonder trail,
forest deep
some words to speak,
mounds in two
next to creek,
falls above
water seeks,
ridge on high
crumbling all,
over time
piece by piece,
flourishing greens
my eyes do find,
growing there
a place to climb,
wooden bridge
rocky path,
valley high
seems at ease,
perhaps it's not
so calm at peace.

Trail zigzags
the elk were here,
meadow high
a place of cheer,

shelter rock
words written there,
woman speaks
of things to share,
I see the snow
rock and ice does glow,
mountain sings
its sight when bright,
melodious soft
I hear in mind,
wondrous music
of a silent kind –
on down the trail
I must go,
feeling light
my feet do lead,
and upon the line
where forest grows,
a feather lays
a hawk I know,
my heart is glad
I came this way,
as on I walk
in light of day.

The lake above
small and calm,
spirit moves
just like a song,
sky above
in evening true,
moon to light
the twilight soon,
riffles roll
from fishy there,
insects fly
they know not where,
peace I find
sweet amends of mind,
near peaks above
I'd like to climb,
hawks two soar
on the wind,

looking down
with thoughts within,
a silence here
calm and fresh,
as in the west
the sun does set,
shadows fold
as night does come,
and down the road
our life does go,
we pass the lake
we see the elk,
to us this all
was more than fun,
valley low
in shadow glow,
steep and green
the forest shows,
as on we go
while nighttime grows.

Volcano sleeps
within its peak,
not long ago
it did not sleep,
roaring wind
fired heat,
bursting land
from high and steep,
clouds did rise
high in sky,
black and filled
with dusty silt,
earth did shake
tremor deep,
tears did flow
for some we weep,
the land now is
coming back,
to spray with hope
new life on slopes,
devastating blast
laid down the growth,

we pass and know
with this we'll cope,
enduring as
we walk through time,
we know inside
love truly shines.

I end this verse
for a spell,
as there is

much more to tell,
and in some future
time and place,
I hope to pick
up pen and write,
another tale
of natures life,
and mountain there
within one's sight.

These poetical lines are from my field notes—a record book carried on the trail—such notes were written then to be later read and expanded upon so as to create the book. It took many drafts and much time and effort to complete this short expression of *The Mountain*—a human experience description in the field of nature—the summer of 1993.

I'd like to note that the Naturalist John Muir, in 1888, also visited Mount Rainier and did comment that the mountain was, "…the most majestic solitary mountain I had ever beheld." I too share his expression, perception, and impression of—the mountain, Mount Rainier.

Places and People ∆∆∆∆∆∆∆∆

BURROUGHS MOUNTAIN: NE slope, named after naturalist, John Burroughs.

EMMONS GLACIER: NE slope, was called White Glacier, is named in honor of S.F. Emmons who with A.D. Wilson, made second successful ascent of Mount Rainier in 1870.

INTER GLACIER: named by Major E.E. Ingraham, when he attempted to ascend but failed 1886.

LITTLE TAHOMA PEAK: named by Prof. J.B. Flett and H.H. Garretson, upon first ascent.

LIBERTY CAP: named by Bailey Willis 1883.

MOUNT RAINIER: named for Admiral Peter Rainier of the British Navy, by Captain George Vancouver, on Tuesday May 8th 1792.

MOUNT RUTH: named in honor of Ruth Knapp, daughter of the prospector who built "Knapp Cabin," at Glacier Basin area.

PEAK SUCCESS (POINT SUCCESS): named by Stevens and Van Trump 1870, on occasion of making first ascent of mountain.

SARVENT GLACIERS: named for Henry M. Sarvent, engineer who made the first detailed map of Mount Rainier.

SUMMER LAND: named by Major E.E. Ingraham 1888.

TIPSOO: tinder for starting a fire, woolly under bark or dry grass. Tipsoo used to flame a spark or glowing coal.

DOCTOR WILLIAM FRASER TOLMIE: 1812-88, during August 29th and September 3rd of 1833 he entered from the northwest corner of the mountain, the first white man to penetrate that region and pinpoint its glaciers. In May of the same year, Fort Nisqually was established, founded by the Hudson Bay Company.

WHITE RIVER: the original Indian name, **SMALOCHO**.

COMMANDER CHARLES WILKES: 1798-1877, in the spring of 1841 then Lieut. Charles Wilkes of the US Exploring Expedition, observed the mountain from Nisqually House and on May 19th of that year sent a contingent under Lt. Robert E. Johnson, over Naches Pass, the first recorded survey made by a white man.   Lt. Robert E. Johnson was likely not the first white man to cross the Cascades, yet he was the first to leave a known record. A contingent of six men, were given 80days to cross over to Fort Colville, Fort Okanogan, and other posts, but returned on July 15 in 57days.

THEODORE WINTHROP*: lived 1828-61; his book *The Canoe and the Saddle* is the first place the Indian name of Mount Rainier appears in print, where he declares the mountain as "Tacoma." His book will remain a classic work describing the Pacific Northwest. Lines of the last paragraph of his book, describes the effect of the region upon him, "…and in all that period while I was so near to Nature, the great lessons of the wilderness deepened into my heart day by day, the hedges of conventionalism withered away from my horizon, and all the pedantries of scholastic thought perished out of my mind forever."

---

*The Canoe and the Saddle, by Theodore Winthrop, Binfords & Mort, Publishers, Portland, Oregon, Nisqually Edition, illustrated, including also a partial vocabulary of the Chinook Jargon; the book was in print of recent.

www.ingramcontent.com/pod-product-compliance
Lightning Source LLC
Chambersburg PA
CBHW061532250726
48657CB00005B/2201